When Sheep Feed the Shepherds

Fun Ways for Churches to Show Their Love for Their Pastors

This title is also available as an eBook from Amazon.com

All rights reserved. No part of this publication may be reproduced, stored in a retrieval system, or transmitted in any form or by any means – electronic, mechanical, photocopy, recording, or any other – except for brief quotations in printed reviews, without the prior permission of the publisher.

Table of Contents

LITTLE SNACKS OF LOVE- WRITE THEM A NOTE! 9
   1. Affirm the Preacher's Kids 12
   2. All Church "Thank You" Letter Project 13
   3. Stuff the Appreciation Jar 14
   4. Community Chest of Cards 15
   5. Recognize Their Personal Wins 16
   6. Send Notes to Staff Family Members 18
   7. Sermon Notes 19
   8. Personal Notes 20
   9. Social Media Avalanche 21

FOOD EXTRAVAGANZA! BIG EVENTS TO FEED THEIR SOUL 23
   10. "And the Award Goes To" 24
   11. Watch the Kids 25
   12. Crazy Good Birthday Party 27
   13. Sharpen the Axe 28
   14. Bonus Like You Mean It 29
   15. We All Scream For Ice Cream 30
   16. Lifetime Achievement Award 31
   17. Pizza Pie, That's Amore 33
   18. Family Day Excursion 34
   19. Show & Tell Lunch 35
   20. BBQ & Blue Jeans 36
   21. This Is Your Life 37

HOME COOKIN'! PERSONAL GIFTS & STUFF YOU CAN DO 39

22. Build a Brag Board 40
23. Life is Short, Eat Dessert First 41
24. Weed the Bed 42
25. Rock Star Treatment 43
26. It's on the Internet 45
27. Spamsgiving 46
28. ABC's of Blessings 47
29. Use Your Words 48
30. Sermon Signs 49
31. Leaf Them, but Not Alone 51

FREE SAMPLES! GIVE A LOT FOR NOTHING AT ALL! 52

32. Workin' at the Car Wash 53
33. Play Ball! Or Golf! Or Tennis! 54
34. It's Personal 55
35. When Momma's Happy 57
36. Silver Screen Story 58
37. Cutest Little Baby 59
38. Work It Out 60
39. And the Survey Says… 61
40. Mow, Mow, Mow the Yard 63
41. Pet Projects 64
42. Picture Mash-Up 65
43. See You in the Funny Papers 66
44. Cartoon Me 67
46. Phone a Friend 70

47. Making Headlines 71
48. Time with the Kids 72
49. Take It When You Want It 73
50. Take the Most Hated Task 75
51. Give Them the Moon 76
52. Roll the Presses 77
53. Hit the Lake House 78
54. Pooch Sit 80
55. Winter Windshield Duty 81
56. Solve a Problem 82
57. Give 'em a Standing "O"! 83
58. Put Me in Coach 84
59. Sticky Notes 86
60. Love Boxer 87

APPETIZERS ARE IN ORDER- INEXPENSIVE IDEAS 88
61. Float Some Java 89
62. Discount Dining 91
63. I Had the Time of My Life 92
64. Feed the Soul 93
65. Best Meal of the Day 94
66. Relaxable 96
67. Random is Good 97
68. Scrapbooking 98
69. Snacktacular 99
70. Drinks are on the House 100
71. Employee of the Month/Year 102

72. Gag Them 103

73. Fill 'er Up 104

74. DJ Pastor 105

75. Reading All Year Long 107

76. Gift Basket of the Month 108

77. Mouse on the Face 109

78. My Other Shirt is a Collar 110

79. Flip Flopper 111

80. Cookies & Fruit & Stuff Oh My 113

81. Marshmallows or Whipped 114

82. Seeing the Silver Screen 115

83. Thirsty? 116

84. Flexible is the New YES! 117

85. Say it with Flowers 119

86. Proclamation & Seal 120

87. Put Their Mug on a Mug 121

88. Gratitude Journal 122

89. Treat Them Like Royalty 123

90. Dropping Off Lunch 124

91. Mighty Morphing Trophy 126

92. Plaque Treatment 127

93. Bring the Midway Home 128

94. Sabbatical 129

95. Making History 131

96. Roll Out the Donuts 132

97. Wall of Famer 133

98. Slinging Web Stuff 134

99. Stocking Up the Good Stuff 135

BELLY UP FOR THE MAIN COURSE! THIS MAY COST A LITTLE ... 136

    100. Smells Like Team Spirit 137

    101. Brand Them 138

    102. Dinner with Leadership 140

    103. You So Fancy 141

    104. Taking Care of Business 143

    105. Showers of Cards 144

    106. Sacking Groceries 145

    107. Bobble Head Pastor 146

    108. Maid in America 148

    109. Personal Assistant for a Day 149

    110. Home Improvement 150

    111. Flip This Office 152

    112. Don't Muzzle the Ox 153

    113. Photo Bombs 154

    114. What's Behind Door #3? 155

    115. Picnic Basket in the Park 157

    116. There's a Gorilla at the Door 158

    117. Calgon, Take Them Away 160

    118. Surprise! 161

    119. It's a Fiesta 162

THE ICING ON THE CAKE! OPEN YOUR WALLET UP WIDE 163

    120. A New Chair 164

    121. Date/Family Night Out 165

122. A Lamp Would Be Cool 167
123. Don't Forget the Lighter 168
124. Donate To Their Cause 169
125. Baseball Cards or Star Trek 170
126. It's An Original 171
127. Helmet Head 173
128. Life Coaching 174
129. Basket Weaving is Nice 176
130. Call the Limo 177
131. Mama Needs a New Pair of Shoes 178

ALPHABET SOUP- ATTITUDES THAT FEED THEIR SOUL 180

INTRODUCTION

God calls all of us to serve in His Kingdom. All of the footing is level at the foot of the cross. But God uses those He calls as pastors and leaders in our local churches to serve Him in a unique way. As shepherds of a local congregation, God sets some apart to spend their lives in walking the fine line between leading and serving.

The life of a pastoral staff member can be challenging. Living in the "fish bowl" of church can be stressful to say the least. Pastors can give and give and give until they are too empty to shepherd their churches, or care for their own families well. Depression and emotional emptiness can attack those God has set aside to lead and care for us. Ministry can become a burden, and service a drudgery. This should never take place.

You can keep this from happening. How, you ask? By simply feeding the souls of your pastoral staff. Encouraging words can restore a soul. Simple notes of encouragement can give them an emotional boost they can draw on for days. Small gifts or acts of kindness have a way of restoring faith, building up hope and showing love in ways you cannot imagine.

So why don't more people do this? Two reasons. First, they just don't think about it. Church members are so used to having their needs met by their pastoral staff they forget that pastors have needs too. The Bible teaches us, "Those who are taught the word of God should provide for their teachers, sharing all good things with them." Galatians 6:6 NLT

It's not only a good thing to do, the Scriptures actually direct us to care for our pastors! God's design is for pastors to care for their church members, and the church members to care for their pastors!

The second reason I believe church members may not show appreciation as often as their pastoral staff members' need it is simply the lack of a plan of specific ways they might show appreciation or love to their pastors. But the Bible challenges each of us, "Dear brothers and sisters, honor those who are your leaders in the Lord's work. They work hard among you and give you spiritual guidance. [13] Show them great respect and wholehearted love because of their work. And live peacefully with each other." I Thessalonians 5:12-13 NLT

Showing your pastoral staff "great respect and wholehearted love" doesn't mean you salute them, or stand when they enter and leave a room. It simply means you make a conscious effort with your words and your actions to show them how much they are loved and respected!" That's what this book is all about! I hope you use it to bless your pastoral staff for years to come!

Page Cole

Little Snacks of Love- Write Them a Note!

1. Affirm the Preacher's Kids

The Purpose
Many Pastor's kids (PK's) feel a lot of pressure to conform. It's hard living in the fishbowl of ministry, where everything you do falls under extra the loving but firm scrutiny of a church family. For some kids, it can breed resentment or detachment from their church family. Don't let this happen. Let your PK's know just how special they are to your church!

The Plan
Write a note to each of their kids telling why they are special and what you admire about them. Be specific and be encouraging. Take the opportunity to affirm their parents as well. Sometimes PK's don't understand just how much a church family and the individual church members value their pastoral staff. Brag on their mom and dad, and the qualities about them you admire.

The Place
U.S. Postage! Don't take the quick, easy way by sending an email. There is a time and place for that, but write an old fashioned letter and mail it to them. In this day and age, it will be something unusual, and something they can keep and treasure for years to come!

The Price
Free! But if you choose to, you can include fun inexpensive gifts as well. A CD, bookmark or a restaurant gift card are just a few ideas you might consider!

2. All Church "Thank You" Letter Project

The Purpose
Pastors do what they do because of their calling, their devotion to God & their love for people. You can let them know how much you appreciate them, and magnify that thanks by spearheading project that invites the entire church family to write notes of thanks to the pastoral staff.

The Plan
Write letters to your pastoral staff. A LOT of letters. No seriously, write a ton of letters. You can provide the blank notes & pens, but it's more personal if you ask church members to provide their own stationary. Be sure and pass out instructions on how and when to deliver the notes.

The Place
You may choose to have a central drop off point for all letters, or encourage individuals to all mail their notes during the same week.

The Price
Free, or really cheap!

3. Stuff the Appreciation Jar

The Purpose
All of us like to know our work makes a difference, and that we are appreciated. Your pastoral staff need this too!

The Plan
Although similar to other note writing suggestions included here, this was is unique in its own way. Challenge church members to think of those things that they appreciate most about his or her character and ministry.

The Place
They can write those notes of appreciation and drop them off in the church lobby in a jar. If there is more than one pastor on staff, have a separate jar for each staff member. Decorate the jars, and be sure a keep a large stock of notecards and pens near each jar!

The Price
Very cheap! Cost of the large jars can be offset by asking groups within the church to provide and decorate the jar for the staff person who leads their ministry. You can put these notes in a nice scrapbook and present them to the pastor at a fellowship or dinner.

4. Community Chest of Cards

The Purpose
Great pastors do more than just minister to their own church and church members. They are actively involved in their local schools, community and businesses. Give people outside your church to thank them.

The Plan
Brainstorm a list of people who interact with your pastor, but who are outside your church family. Ask your pastors' wife to help you with this list. Approach those individuals with your idea about thank you notes, and see if they are willing to participate. If they are, provide them with stationary to write their notes. At the time you drop off the stationary, offer to come back and pick up their complete notes.

The Place
You may need to put a team together, since this project will involve travelling out to people in the community, once to deliver and once to pick up the notes. For extra measure, get a small desktop "chest" to put his new treasures in. Be sure and invite those kind people who wrote notes to attend!

The Price
Very inexpensive! Free in most instances! Way cheap!

5. Recognize Their Personal Wins

The Purpose
Sometimes it's wonderful when the church recognizes what we call "personal wins"! Write them a note and let them see that you noticed, and you're impressed!

The Plan
Those happen when your pastor runs his first 5K, gets his black belt, or graduates from school. Maybe they've lost weight, published a book or bought a new home- it doesn't matter, as long as you can celebrate it with them! When they've achieved a notable milestone outside the office, whether it has anything to do with the church or not, celebrate with them! You can do anything to celebrate- decorate their office or car, send them a flower, fruit or candy bouquet, or put an ad in the paper! Celebrate with them!

The Place
This can take place at the location of their accomplishment (finish line of a 5K, or their local dojo!)

The Price
Free, all it will take is your time and some heart!

6. Send Notes to Staff Family Members

The Purpose
Love on your pastor by loving on their family, and letting them know how much the service, love and commitment of your pastor means.

The Plan
When a pastor has to go out of town, works long hours or Saturdays, or is taken away from their family for work-related reasons, why not write a note thanking them! Beyond that, you could also send flowers or gift cards for dinner out to the pastor's spouse, acknowledging their sacrifice and thanking them for it.

The Place
Be sure to call and give advance notice to the pastors family. This is especially important if you're having food delivered or dropping something off at their house while the pastor is away.

The Price
Encouragements are always free, and you pick if you want to do something a little or a lot extra to show appreciation.

7. Sermon Notes

The Purpose
Pastors work long, hard hours preparing the sermons they deliver to their flock. It's incredibly encouraging to them to see people actually paying attention and taking notes!

The Plan
Choose one thing from each sermon your pastor preaches this month and send a note expressing how you benefited from it. He may pass out when he finds out that you not only listened, but you wrote something down and then repeated it back to him! Beyond the notes you took, consider asking some follow up questions or sharing with him how you are implementing what you learned from his sermons into your daily life.

The Place
This one is great when done in person! Have your sermon notes on hand to show him, and when a hug follows the thank you, it's even better!

The Price
Totally free, but priceless! Your time is the only cost, but you can't buy this kind of blessing!

8. Personal Notes

The Purpose
Most pastors have a box, file or drawer full of the notes people have written them. These are a lifeline during times of stress or challenge! You need to be a part of filling that box!

The Plan
Be liberal, and be specific about what you're thankful for! This is no run of the mill, generic thank you note. This is reminding him of a time he helped you through a rough patch. It's recollecting the good times you shared in ministry. It's a celebration on paper of a faith journey shared!

The Place
Take your time writing this note. Write it, rewrite it, and then write it again so that it conveys your heart for them. Hand the signed envelope to them following a busy service, hug their neck and leave them to read it alone later. It is better that way… no one likes to cry in front of people.

The Price
No cost, but cherished forever!
Most pastors have box, file or drawer full of the notes people have written them. These are a lifeline during times of stress or challenge! Be liberal, and be specific about what you're thankful for!

9. Social Media Avalanche

The Purpose
More and more pastors are staying in touch with their church through social media. Take advantage of his favorite social media platform to make him feel appreciated!

The Plan
If you want it to be a surprise, you'll need to privately communicate with as many people as you can to send their own thank you note via social media before the big avalanche day. It can be just as effective to promote the event through other mediums, and not try to make it a surprise. Word can spread faster and farther if you're blitzing the internet to promote this event!

The Place
The digital superhighway! Facebook, Twitter, Instagram- it doesn't matter as long as you can gets a lot of people to sign on and show their thanks!

The Price
Free, of course! With so much weirdness and junk on social media, take advantage of this free medium to make your pastors' day!

Food Extravaganza! Big Events to Feed Their Soul

10. "And the Award Goes To"

The Purpose
Awards are cool. Kids aren't the only ones who love them either. Use an "awards ceremony" motif to recognize the sacrifices and service of your pastoral staff.

The Plan
Get a group of creative people together to brainstorm for creative award names, clever "trophies' to represent those awards, and funny and unique ways to present them to the pastoral staff.

The Place
You can choose to do these within the context of a dessert fellowship, a regularly scheduled mid-week dinner, or turn it into a full blown production! The bigger the event, the larger your team of volunteers will need to be, and the greater the expense.

The Price
This will vary greatly based on the type of venue you choose to present the awards, and the type of awards. Gifts are more expensive than a homemade trophy, and piggybacking this event on the midweek dinner is cheaper than having a special church-wide dinner. Choose what works best for your church.

11. Watch the Kids

The Purpose
A night completely free of church events is a treasure to a pastor's family. But for a pastor and spouse to go out, it can get expensive when you add the cost of child care to the mix. You can remove that burden so they can enjoy a night out alone.

The Plan
Be very intentional about your offer to babysit. "Hey, if you ever want me to babysit, let me know!" is NOT intentional. Instead, try, "Hey, I'd love to babysit for you guys on a Friday or Saturday night, this week or next! Can I call you tomorrow to see which of those nights works best for you?" For many pastors, you almost have to corner them into taking advantage of such a gracious offer. So put them in the corner!

The Place
You can offer to babysit at their house, or offer to take the kids out on an adventure to the movies or the park! Either way works great!

The Price
Free, of course! If you want to do something special for or with the kids you are babysitting, that cost could be minimal.

12. Crazy Good Birthday Party

The Purpose
This is not meant to replace a family celebration, but to do something over the top for them in addition to that event.

The Plan
Go all out. Party hats, party games, cake and ice cream are all in order! Invite other staff, church members and friends. Have great music, lots of laughs, and a themed decoration can be great too! Just because they are getting older doesn't mean they have to grow up, does it?! Another fun option here is simply to take them to lunch with the other staff, and buy the pastor's lunch. Have the other guests bring fun, inexpensive gifts to top it off!

The Place
Parties are fun no matter where they are! Have it as a surprise during the workday at the church! Rent a room at a restaurant and make it a dinner party! Bring their spouse in on it, and have everyone show up at the pastor's house one evening!

The Price
This event can be fairly inexpensive if it happens at the church, and the duties for decorations, food and activities are spread out among a group of people! Buying lunch at a staff lunch party is fairly inexpensive too!

13. Sharpen the Axe

The Purpose
Sometimes our pastors get so busy taking care of the needs of the church they forget to care for their own. One critical area is their own personal and professional growth. Forcing them to go away to a conference or workshop can be both refreshing and educational!

The Plan
It's important to know what kinds of training events they would benefit from. This event is most effective if the pastor is brought in on the choosing and scheduling of the retreat.

The Place
Although there is value for a pastor to participate in local learning events, this activity is designed to get him out of town. He not only gets to "sharpen his axe" by learning in a new environment, but he also gets to relax a little!

The Price
Depending on the length of the conference, the distance and travel costs, and other miscellaneous expenditures this can be a little pricey. But your pastor is worth it, right?!

14. Bonus Like You Mean It

The Purpose
This suggestion is aimed at people in the church who serve on Personnel or Budget teams that impact the compensation of the pastor. Beyond paying a fair salary, consider bonuses along the way.

The Plan
Annual evaluations are a great time to look back across pastoral performance over the past year. But they are also the best time to look ahead! Help your pastor set realistic but challenging goals in the coming year, and bonus him with cash or time off when those goals are reached!

The Place
If you're an elder, deacon, committee or team member that influences the compensation of your staff, then your meetings are where this discussion needs to being. Your hearts make the difference. Dream big, and bless accordingly.

The Price
Cash bonuses don't have to huge, but they ought to be large enough to matter! Time or other bonuses ought to be worthy as well. Maybe a bonus is a new set of golf clubs, or a membership at the local gym. Have fun with it.

15. We All Scream For Ice Cream

The Purpose
Sometimes the world is a mean ugly place. When that happens, two things always make it better. Prayer, and ice cream! Put a smile on their face with an ice cream sundae!

The Plan
Do a little homework beforehand to find out the favorite flavors of ice cream of our pastoral staff! Gather the toppings, disposable bowls and silverware (no one wants to do the dishes!), and have a Sundae building party!

The Place
The church office is a great place for this! It breaks up the busyness and monotony of the work week, and the staff will feel incredibly appreciated and loved!

The Price
Ice cream and toppings are fairly cheap. Cut loose with the extra cash to buy the whipped cream and nuts!

16. Lifetime Achievement Award

The Purpose
The purpose here is two-fold. First, you're recognizing the milestone achievements of your current pastor or pastors, and that's an awesome thing! The second purpose? I'll tell you later!

The Plan
Host a party to recognize the very best achievements of your staff. Highlight the stuff that's really important… Lives they have touched, sacrifices they've made, obstacles they've overcome. Skip the number crunching, statistics and other boring trivia.

The Place
Remember that second purpose I mentioned? Well here it is! If you will have this party and recognize one current pastoral staff member every time you hire a new pastoral staff member, you'll not only recognize someone who deserves it, but you'll also be setting the standard for what real success looks like for the new person!

The Price
Dinners can be pricey, but there's nothing that says you can't do this on a shoestring budget… literally. Have the church hostess fix hamburgers and shoestring fries, and cookies for dessert! It will be awesome, and won't break the bank in doing it!

17. Pizza Pie, That's Amore

The Purpose
It brings out the creativity in inventors, the memories with old friends, and the celebration after winning a big game. What is it? This magical stuff that unites enemies and brings a smile to the face of children... its pizza! Use it to bless your staff

The Plan
If you're going to order pizza, then be sneaky and find out what kinds of pizza they like best. Don't forget the drinks, plates and napkins—but no forks!

The Place
You can load the pastoral staff up and take them out to the local buffet, or bring it by the office one day just to say thanks for all they do! If you go to a pizza place with an arcade, be sure and give them each some quarters to have fun with!

The Price
Pizza is fairly cheap, and nearly every pizza place offers coupons and deals. Shop around to get the best deal.

18. Family Day Excursion

The Purpose
One of the greatest gifts you can give your pastors is to help them make quality memories with their families and with each other! Set aside one afternoon a month to give them something to look forward to!

The Plan
Brainstorm a list of day trips that you could send them on. To make this experience special, you can provide the picnic lunches and snacks for them to take with them. Go old school, and buy some disposable cameras for each person, and have them take real pictures for their scrapbook!

The Place
You might help them have a day at the beach, make a zoo trip, visit the local aquarium, spend a day at the fair, take canoe rides or go on a hiking trip are just a few ideas!

The Price
Cost will vary from free to moderately expensive, depending on how big you want to go. It's OK to balance these trips between free and not-so-free.

19. Show & Tell Lunch

The Purpose
Building community among your pastoral staff is something that benefits them and the church. Some of that community happens naturally, but develops to a deeper level with intentional efforts like this.

The Plan
Set aside one workday per month for a staff lunch, and call it "Show & Tell" lunch! Have each person bring something from home (something they love to do, a hobby, interest or talent) and "show & tell" it to their fellow staff members!

The Place
Cater lunch in to the church, and have the staff eat and share their "stuff" after everyone gets their plate filled!

The Price
Low cost lunch is the only expense here, unless you also wanted to do a fun door prize or drawing just to make it a little more exciting!

20. BBQ & Blue Jeans

The Purpose
BBQ just shouts "let's have a party!" Providing casual celebrations for your pastoral staff to hang out, relax and enjoy life is a great way to show them you care!

The Plan
Talk to your staff about having a "Western Day" at church and follow it up with an all Church BBQ. During this event, have some fun "cowboy competition" events involving your pastoral staff! Present them with gift cards to their favorite BBQ or Western wear store!

The Place
This event can take place anywhere, but if you are able to reserve rodeo arena, it adds to the fun and feel of the event! If you want to make this a "staff only" event, then cater in to the church office during the workweek!

The Price
BBQ can be expensive, so be prepared if this is a church-wide event. You can always invite people to bring sides & desserts to lower the cost. But don't skimp on the gifts to show your appreciation to your pastoral staff.

21. This Is Your Life

The Purpose
This event is a great way to recognize milestones of service. When pastors spend 5, 10, 20 years or more at one location, they deserve to be blessed. An event that highlights snap shots of their ministry and its impact is a fun way to do that!

The Plan
Contact as many people as you can who have been involved in his/her ministry, and invite them back for the event. Gather pictures, video and testimonials to remind them and the people what a difference their ministry has made over the years. Have a fun picture booth as well for people to take fun pictures with the pastoral staff during a fellowship time following the program.

The Place
You may choose to wrap this around a meal as well, although it's not necessary. You might also replace an evening worship time with this event.

The Price
Make the night memorable. Thank you letters, from both present and past members can be compiled into a nice scrapbook. Consider a money tree or love offering as a way to show appreciation. Give people several weeks beforehand to donate to this gift, and find a creative way to present the money.

Home Cooking'! Personal Gifts & Stuff You Can Do

22. Build a Brag Board

The Purpose
Create a board where anyone in the office or church can post "brags" about the pastoral staff!

The Plan
Purchase a simple bulletin board, and decorate it with any theme you like! Leave space for newspaper articles, thank you notes or kids projects bragging on and showing appreciation for the pastoral staff.

The Place
Don't hide this in the church office, but get permission to put it up somewhere in the church where both members and pastoral staff can see it regularly. Encourage people regularly, through announcements, newsletters and small groups to make time to post things on the "Brag Board"!

The Price
The initial cost of buying the board and decorating it should be your only expenses here.

23. Life is Short, Eat Dessert First

The Purpose
There's just something wonderful about bringing someone a surprise dessert! Cake... pie... cookies... ice cream... even popsicles... it's all GOOD! Make your pastors day by dropping a delicious dessert off to be devoured!

The Plan
Do a little investigative work, and if possible find out what his/her favorite dessert is. If necessary, bring plates or bowls, forks or spoons, and a can of whipped cream is always a nice touch!

The Place
Surprise them right after lunch at the office, or drop it off to them at the end of the workday so they can take it home and share it with their family.

The Price
This can be very inexpensive if you're able to make the dessert yourself. Homemade desserts always taste best anyway, and if you can personalize it by writing a message on a cake, or decorating a happy face on the cookies it's that much better!

24. Weed the Bed

The Purpose
Most people hate weeds. More people hate pulling weeds from their flowerbeds. So why not take this unpleasant task off of the "to do" list of your favorite pastor?

The Plan
This activity is one that is best served as a surprise when it's completely finished! You don't want your pastor to feel guilty and try to help, so plan it for a time where you know he/she won't be returning home for several hours.

The Place
Determine exactly which flower beds at their home you have the time or ability to care for. You don't want to make decisions for them that they might not appreciate, like changing out their shrubs or flowers. Your goal is to clean and enhance, not completely redesign their flower beds.

The Price
Pulling weeds is free! Mulch is not that expensive, and if you do feel like you can add some flowers or shrubs they will approve of, there may be some moderate expenses to pull this one off.

25. Rock Star Treatment

The Purpose
If you or someone that can help you has some crazy good video skills, then offer to shoot and produce a fun music video involving your pastoral staff! Pastors typically love to have fun, and don't mind being a little silly!

The Plan
This is YOUR idea. Give them plenty of warning time to prepare, and then show up with a plan, costumes, and all the equipment necessary to shoot the video.

The Place
Depending on the song and the topic, you'll want to choose the spot or spots for shooting the video well. Don't take the easy route and shoot the entire thing in the church office. If it's a country song, find a barn. If it's an upbeat pop song, choose a unique urban location! Have fun!

The Price
If you have the people with the right skills, this fun event can be pulled off for a relatively low cost. Borrow costumes, props and other things needed for the video.

26. It's on the Internet

The Purpose
You know your pastoral staff are incredible people. Now it's time for the world to know it! If you have a blog, then use a blog post to tell the world just how amazing they are!

The Plan
This post does NOT have to be exclusively information from you alone. Do the work to interview people, gather pictures of your pastor with church members or doing ministry activities, and include those in your blog post. Don't forget to do the follow up work by promoting the blog article so that as many people as possible get to read it!

The Place
You are probably not the only person in your church that has a blog. Why not coordinate an effort to encourage everyone in your church that has a blog to write their own affirming posts and post pics with the pastor during the same day or week!?

The Price
It's Free! Free shouldn't mean that it's not quality though! Put in the time, effort and prayer to write a blog that truly affirms them and their ministry.

27. Spamsgiving

The Purpose
Email boxes of your pastoral staff are not only filled with spam, but also emails filled with complaints, criticisms and challenging issues for your pastoral staff to deal with. Why not take advantage of email to send encouraging notes, affirmations and stories about how their ministry has impacted your life!

The Plan
Think several days about what you want to say. Fill the email with personal stories about how you have experienced blessings from their ministry. Include stories about how you've seen their ministry impact others as well.

The Place
Send the email to their church email address. Invite others to join you by sending their own emails, creating an "email avalanche" of love!

The Price
It's totally FREE!!! Spammers fill the email boxes of all of us with offers of Botox, wonder cures and other junk we don't want or need. Show some love that costs NOTHING to your pastor and his email box!

28. ABC's of Blessings

The Purpose
Sometimes your staff just needs a list... a list from you of all the qualities, character traits and talents you see in them!

The Plan
It's simple to do. Take a sheet of notebook paper, and write out the alphabet, with only on letter per line. Then choose words that start with each letter of the alphabet, an "alphabet soup" of compliments and encouragement!

The Place
After the list has been made, then dress it up. Rewrite the list on nice stationary, or use a word processor to create a document fit for framing!

The Price
The only cost here is if you actually decide to frame the document... and you should!

29. Use Your Words

The Purpose
The power of the spoken word is immeasurable. The thoughtful encouragement, gracious compliment, well timed gratitude can brighten a pastor's day, and provide a wave of hope and joy that can last for weeks or months!

The Plan
This is best done face to face. Be sincere, and offer your thanks for ministry tasks performed well, or for the character trait they possess that you admire most. Remind them of the positive, eternal impact they have on you and on your church.

The Place
There are times where this should be done one-on-one, but other opportunities come where you can give thanks in front of several people, or at an all-church event.

The Price
Cost here is free… value of this thank you is simply beyond measuring. Speech really is free. Be an American! Use your free speech to honor your pastor!

30. Sermon Signs

The Purpose
Sometimes your pastoral staff needs you to be a player on the team. Other times, they need you to be a cheerleader as they lead the team! Have fun cheering them on.

The Plan
Using poster board and markers, make some signs that say, "Amen!", "That's Right!", "Great job!" & "Love You!" You don't want to interrupt an important moment in a sermon. Maybe at the beginning of the service, or at the end of the service, you and your other "sign bearers" could show some poster board love!

The Place
Make sure you and the others are positioned strategically around the auditorium, so that not only can the pastor see your signs, but that others in the congregation can see them too!

The Price
Poster board and markers are cheap! Have fun with this! If you want to really go big, use some glitter and glue too!

31. Leaf Them, but Not Alone

The Purpose
Fall is a beautiful time of the year, but in a yard with a lot of trees, raking and bagging leaves can eat up a large chunk of the small amount of weekend free time your pastor has. Why not show some appreciation by gathering a group and tackling this task for him?

The Plan
Gather a group of people so that you can attack his/her yard, and quickly rake, bag and haul off the leaves from the entire yard. Call it a "Rake & Run", and do this for all members of your church pastoral staff in one Saturday!

The Place
Have everyone meet at the church, and then go in a group to the pastoral staff member's home. Be sure someone has a truck, trailer or both so that you can haul away the full bags of leaves!

The Price
With every person involved bringing their own rake and box of heavy duty leaf bags, this event turns out to be free, or pretty close to free!

FREE SAMPLES! GIVE A LOT FOR NOTHING AT ALL!

32. Workin' at the Car Wash

The Purpose
With the ever growing list of things to take care of at the church and with family, washing the car can quickly fall to the bottom of the list of priorities for your pastor. It's not that they don't care how the care looks. They just care about you more. Why not take care of this task so he/she doesn't have to?

The Plan
Two options here. First, if you can sneak a second set of keys from a spouse, then get them and do a wash and detail on the car as a surprise. If that doesn't work, option two is the direct approach. Let the pastor know what you want to do, and don't take no for an answer. Take the keys away, and don't bring it back till it's spotless!

The Place
You can pay to have the car cleaned and detailed if you want to. Another fun option is to involve a group of people and give everyone a piece of the opportunity to bless your pastor!

The Price
If you pay to have the car washed and detailed, then it could get a little expensive. If you have a crew that can wash, wax & vacuum, then it's free!

33. Play Ball! Or Golf! Or Tennis!

The Purpose
Want to give your pastor a really cool gift? How about one part fun, one part fresh air, and one part friendship? It's awesome! Get them outside having fun doing something they love with people they enjoy!

The Plan
If you don't already know what recreational sports your pastor enjoys, then find out! Once you know, then make plans to do it with them! Kayaking his thing? Then rent some boats! Playing golf his "go to" for relaxation? Then reserve a tee time!

The Place
Make sure that you've covered all of the details necessary so that your pastor just walks in and has fun! Gather the equipment and make the reservations so that all they need to show up and have fun!

The Price
The cost for this event varies greatly. If your pastor loves to hike or go jogging, then it's free! If instead he's more of a golfer or skydiver, there may be some expense involved.

34. It's Personal

The Purpose
The gift that speaks the loudest is the gift that touches the heart. Find a way to touch their heart.

The Plan
This option involves creating a very personal connection between you and your pastor. Find something that means a great deal to you... a favorite book, a special sports item, or a piece of memorabilia that has special value for you. Then give it to them. It's that simple.

The Place
Don't make a big show with lots of people around. This gift has the greatest impact if you find a special time with just you, or you and a few close friends to give this gift away.

The Price
If you already own the item you plan to give away, there's really know financial cost here. There is a significant cost as you give away something very special. This special event shouldn't be done flippantly, or often. Choose wisely.

35. When Momma's Happy

The Purpose
The quality of a pastoral ministry is in direct proportion to the quality and joy of his or her home life. Find a way to bring joy to your pastor by bringing joy to his/her spouse.

The Plan
There are so many things you can do to make the spouse of your pastor happy. It could be as simple as taking her to lunch, having a group of ladies take her to dinner and a movie, or a homemade spa day!

The Place
This event is best conceived in "group think". Get a group of your pastor's spouses best friends together, and have them brainstorm a list of ways to make her day.

The Price
Most of the things that will mean the most are free! Your pastor's wife will love being loved on by you and your friends giving your time and your hearts to her, if only for an evening!

36. Silver Screen Story

The Purpose
Everyone has a secret fantasy to see their name up in lights, their story on the silver screen! Make it happen for your pastor... true story, or fictional embellishment, make some movie magic!

The Plan
Gather some creative geniuses, and come up with a script. Your video extravaganza could involve putting actual still shots of your pastor into a video production. Another option is a more "fictional" approach, especially if you have people with technical and video editing skills. Make a super hero tale, or a melodrama, or a hilarious comedy. Just make it spectacular!

The Place
Any place can become a movie set... the church, the pastor's home, fun and unique locations around your city. For that matter, with a little special effects magic, your pastor could be on the deck of a starship or deep in a tropical jungle! Make it happen!

The Price
This event is free if you have the people with the necessary expertise! Lights, camera, ACTION!

37. Cutest Little Baby

The Purpose
Who doesn't love to have their baby and childhood pictures plastered all over for the world to see? OK, but it will be fun anyway!

The Plan
Work with their spouse or family to gather several different pictures of each of your pastoral staff, and use them to create a poster or mural of each of them. Be sure that you scan all pictures digitally and then create new copies, returning the original pics as quickly as possible.

The Place
These would be great placed in your main church lobby or church fellowship hall. Anywhere you can get lots of people to see the pictures is a great place to display them!

The Price
Not only can you do this event free, but you can turn it into a "Cutest Baby Contest", and have people vote with change. Donate the proceeds to any mission or church building campaign.

38. Work It Out

The Purpose
The stress and time restraints of ministry can prevent pastors from getting the regular exercise they need to stay healthy and happy. You can help them have the consistent accountability and encouragement to make exercise a priority.

The Plan
Determine what schedule works best for both of you. Early mornings, late afternoons or even over the lunch hour are options for a regular workout appointment.

The Place
This can stay the same or change to keep it interesting. You can lift weights, jog, swim or walk. Any of these are great activities to get the heart rate up and build muscle tone!

The Price
Most activities related to getting exercise can be done for free. At most you may have a small monthly fee for a gym membership, but do your pastor and yourself a favor... pick up the cost for both memberships. It will do your heart good!

39. And the Survey Says…

The Purpose
Old fashioned game night with several couples in someone's home is a great way to build relationships and have some real fun! Next time you're planning one of these, invite a pastoral staff member and their spouse to be a part!

The Plan
Invite several couples over for a potluck or cook out dinner. Make sure that your guest list includes some people your pastoral staff member knows, and some they don't know. It gives them a chance to build on old relationships while enriching their lives by introducing them to new folks as well.

The Place
Your home is a great place for people to let down their guard and just relax and be themselves. If your home is not big enough, then talk to a friend who has a home that is big enough.

The Price
Game night is a free event, especially if you ask everyone to bring a potluck dish for the meal. If you want to spice it up a bit, then make your party food a "theme night", and ask everyone to bring either Mexican/Italian/Chinese food.

40. Mow, Mow, Mow the Yard

The Purpose
Mowing the yard is hot, sweaty and dirty work. Although some people enjoy mowing their yard, most would rather someone else take this task off of their list! Why not bless your pastoral staff by having them come home to a manicured yard?!

The Plan
If you're going to take this task on, do it with excellence. Make sure that the yard is mowed evenly, grass bagged, and use a weed eater to trim around the trees and fences to give the yard a sharp and professionally done look.

The Place
Obviously the place needs to be your pastor's yard! For a nice touch, make a yard sign that says, "Yard mowed by people who love their pastor!" and place it near the street where all his neighbors can see it!

The Price
A little gas and a little weed eater string, and a pound or two of sweat and effort is all this event costs!

41. Pet Projects

The Purpose
You expect your pastoral staff to love your church, and to work hard to love its people and fulfill its mission. They do this well. But they also have other passions and pastimes you can support them in!

The Plan
The easiest way to find out what projects they wish they had time for, or organizations they love to support is to ask them. Once that's settled, then this becomes an HR issue. Ask your Personnel Team to build in time off to the compensation package of your pastoral staff to allow them time away to work in these areas, without it affecting their vacation or conference time.

The Place
If it's a personal project, make sure that they have the time and necessary space to pursue it uninterrupted with the normal details and busyness of their regular commitments. If it's serving an organization, insure that the pastor isn't out any money to participate.

The Price
The cost is free. Your pastor will still get his "regular job" done, and most likely done better, as you've fed a part of his soul that might have otherwise gone hungry! A happy soul leads to greater productivity and joy in ministry!

42. Picture Mash-Up

The Purpose
Memories are the currency of life's wealthiest people. Make your pastor one of the richest people in town with this project.

The Plan
Put the word out, via email, mail, texts, phone calls and social media for any fun pictures that families have of themselves, and especially if they have pictures of themselves with the pastor. Have a deadline to have all pictures turned in, either in print or electronically.

The Place
There are tons of ways to make this happen. If you want to do something homemade, then make sure you make quality print copies of all of the pictures you gather, and then return the originals back to their owners. Another option is to use services like www.shutterfly.com, www.snapfish.com, or www.picaboo.com to have a sharp, professional picture book printed.

The Price
A homemade project is very inexpensive, but even the professional books can cost under $20! Go for it!

43. See You in the Funny Papers

The Purpose
Every now & then, we all just need to laugh! Every person has a role in the body of Christ, and you can be the funny bone.

The Plan
This takes some planning and patience to find just the right comic. Find something that reminds you of your pastor, or a situation in your church. If you can find a cartoon that mirrors a point he made in a sermon, then it's a double bonus, because you'll be showing him that you actually listen!

The Place
Before you put the comic in an envelope, you might consider editing it! Put names of other staff members next to characters inside the cartoon, or add your own special artistic touches!

The Price
If you already subscribe to a newspaper, then there's actually no cost involved for you at all! If your pastor has a special affection for any specific comic strip, check your local bookstore for a compilation book as a gift!

44. Cartoon Me

The Purpose
Help your pastor take a light hearted look at himself. The world can be a serious place, and every now and then, even pastors need to lighten up!

The Plan
There are several ways to do this. You can hire someone to draw a caricature of your pastor. You can also hire someone on www.fiverr.com or www.freelancer.com, or a variety of other websites, send them a picture of your pastor, and have them draw a personalized caricature.

The Place
When you have the caricature drawn, be sure to have the artist include some "context". If your pastor is a golfer, have the caricature drawn of your pastor in a humorous setting on the golf course.

The Price
This is not nearly as expensive as you might think. You can spend anywhere from $5 to $50 and get a nice quality caricature! With just a little more cash, you can pick up a nice frame to display the picture!

45. Paying at the Car Wash

The Purpose
So many people are pulling at your pastor with genuine and sometimes pressing needs. When life is at its most hectic, keeping a clean car is at the bottom of the priority list. You can take care of this!

The Plan
Find a way to "borrow" the car. You can usually get their keys from their spouse. Do this during a window of time where you're certain they won't be using their car, so when they return to their car it's a sparkling surprise!

The Place
You can take their car to your home, clean it right there at the church, or if you want to spring for a few quarters, take it to the local self-serve car wash! Don't forget to vacuum and do the floor mats!

The Price
This one is totally free if you put in all the elbow grease! So grease up those elbows and go for it!

46. Phone a Friend

The Purpose
Sometimes ministers wonder if their efforts and prayers ever make a difference. One phone call from you can chase that crazy idea from their mind!

The Plan
Prepare for this call. Take a few minutes to sit down and make a list of the ways this pastor and their ministry has impacted your life and your family. That way you have a cheat sheet close at hand for your call, and you don't leave out any of the good stuff!

The Place
Plan for a time where your pastor is least likely to be interrupted during your call. When you call, ask if it's a good time to visit. If it's not, then call back later.

The Price
Phone calls are totally free. Your time is totally free. The effort to make a list of their life changing impact is so little. The impact your call will have on their day and on their ministry??? Priceless!

47. Making Headlines

The Purpose
Many churches have either a printed or a digital church newsletter. This can be a fantastic tool for shouting to the world how much your staff means to you and to the church!

The Plan
Find out who is in charge of your church newsletter or bulletin. Get approval to have a section of it dedicated to highlighting a staff member, and then gather all of the fun, unique and celebratory information and pictures you can find! Don't dump the project on anyone else... you do the heavy lifting on gathering the material, and leave it to the right person to do the layout.

The Place
The church newsletter is the best location for this, but if your church doesn't do a weekly or monthly newsletter, then either the Sunday bulletin, or an insert to put in the bulletin is just as meaningful!

The Price
There shouldn't be any cost here except your time and love/sweat equity in gathering up all the pictures and information for the special staff feature!

48. Time with the Kids

The Purpose
When a church calls a staff person, they are not calling the entire family on staff. However, their entire family is affected by the heavy workload and crazy schedules of ministry. Make a way for them to have some extra family time!

The Plan
If necessary, run this through proper committee or leadership group to get it approved. Then surprise the staff person with the gift that you can't purchase... the gift of time! Make sure that you give a special day off that they might normally have to spend vacation time for, like during Spring break or a day their kids are out of school.

The Place
Create a fun certificate or proclamation to present to the pastoral staff member. Whether it's presented during a special service or event, or an informal gift given in the church office, it will truly be one of their most treasured moments.

The Price
Time off in a one day increment costs the church nothing, and in fact will multiply the effectiveness and passion for ministry of other days worked by the minister!

49. Take It When You Want It

The Purpose
Although this is very similar to "Time with the Kids", this day of free time is unique, because it's basically a free day to be taken at the discretion of the minister, for whatever they want!

The Plan
This gift certificate can be given as a stand-alone gift, or coupled with a bonus or announcement regarding their compensation for the next budget year!

The Place
Have a little fun with how you deliver this gift! Put the certificate on a silver platter, write on butcher paper and hang it as a banner in the office, or have it delivered by a singing telegram! Just make it a celebration!

The Price
Days off don't truly cost anything. It's especially a good gift for churches that are struggling with finances or have limited ministry dollars to show appreciation for their staff.

50. Take the Most Hated Task

The Purpose
All of us have tasks that we avoid like the plague. They are the jobs that we put off as long as possible, or ignore altogether, hoping they will go away. Your pastor is no exception! Why not take one of those tasks and do it yourself as a gift?

The Plan
Find out from the other staff or from a family member of his what some of those "dreaded tasks" for your pastor might be. Determine which one or how many you can do for them as a love gift of service!

The Place
Keep this activity a secret until the job is done! Most pastors don't receive help well, and they most certainly don't want to dump their most dreaded tasks on someone else! Once you've completed the job, write a simple note letting them know what you've done, and how much you appreciate them!

The Price
A pinch of creativity, a smidgen of sneakiness, and a little effort on part are the only things you'll spend here!

51. Give Them the Moon

The Purpose
Your pastoral staff do such for you and your church. You would give them the moon if you could. Well, maybe you can! You can name a star after them!

The Plan
A simple search on the internet yields a number of websites that will name a star after your favorite pastor, and provide a certificate with all of the important information about the star! Or better yet, pick a star out of the night sky, create your own "authentic certificate", and present it to them! It's a fun way to let your pastor know how special they are!

The Place
Have your pastor and his spouse over for dinner one night. Present the certificate after dinner, and be prepared with a telescope to show them in the night sky where the newly named star is!

The Price
If you create your own certificate, there's no cost at all! If you choose to use an online site like www.nameastarlive.com or www.star-registration.com it could cost $20 to $60!

52. Roll the Presses

The Purpose
Local newspapers are always on the hunt for two things- great stories and good advertisers! You can use one or both of these needs as a way to highlight what a great pastor you have!

The Plan
Everyone has a story. You just have to dig and gather the best parts of it here, to be able to pass them on to your local paper. If your church regularly advertises in the local paper, they will more than likely be open to doing a side story like this as a favor to one of their advertisers! If they aren't interested, consider recruiting a business owner in your church to sponsor an "ad space" where you could post an article promoting your amazing pastor!

The Place
When big events in the life of your pastor take place, you're more likely to get front page billing. Events like long tenures, books published or building projects meet that criteria. But wherever the article falls in the paper, it's still there if you can get it there!

The Price
News stories are free! Sponsored space is free! Make it happen! You can do it… for free!

53. Hit the Lake House

The Purpose
Do you or someone you know own a lake house, a cabin in the woods or even a time share at a condo? A week or weekend in those surroundings would be a cool gift to your pastor and family!

The Plan
Make sure the destination is actually something that would be enjoyable! Your pastor doesn't need time off to spend in a ratty trailer with no utilities, or a cabin in bad need of repairs. Find quality digs, and go with that! If you don't have them yourself, research it among your church family until you find someone that does!

The Place
Its best if the retreat matches your pastors' preferences. If he's a beach bum, then a condo on the coast. If he's a woodsy kind of person, then a cabin on the lake will make his trip memorable!

The Price
Believe it or not, this can almost always be free, since so many people have a friend, family member or church member who owns something like this. It's your job to convince them to offer the time to your pastor! Go for it!

54. Pooch Sit

The Purpose
Pets are an important part of our lives. But in addition to providing companionship and love for us, pets can also be a responsibility that burdens our time and keep us tied down to the home front. You can lift that responsibility from your pastor and family by becoming a pet sitter for them!

The Plan
Be direct. Offer your services to them as the pet sitter, so they can have some much needed time away, without worrying whether their pet(s) care is being handled! A shorter, easier version of this gift is to offer to walk their pet, or take it for an evening!

The Place
There are a couple of ways to help with this task. Make the offer to go by their home to provide care, or to take their pet to your home while the pastor and family are away. Make sure they are fed, watered, exercised and loved on!

The Price
Totally free way for you to express your affection for your pastor and family! Doggone it, just do it!

55. Winter Windshield Duty

The Purpose
Everyone hates the dreaded job of scraping ice and snow from their windshield! It's cold and blustery outside, and you can protect your pastor from this frigid task by doing it for him!

The Plan
Get a good ice scraper and beat your pastor to the task. When he arrives at his vehicle let him find a freshly scraped windshield, side windows and back window!

The Place
There are more than one places to make this gift happen! Time your window scraping so that as he gets to his car to head to work, or as he goes to his car to leave work, he is pleasantly surprised by the sight of freshly cleaned windows!

The Price
You'll end up with a cold nose and chilly hands, but you can count on your warm heart to cheer you up!

56. Solve a Problem

The Purpose
Sometimes pastors are challenged by worry or stress over issues that are beyond their ability to solve or remedy. What if you could spearhead an effort to fix that problem for them?

The Plan
In simple conversation with your pastor, find out what that problem or stressful issue is. Once you're clear on what the problem is, then spend some time in prayer and fasting to find out how God could use you or your efforts to find a solution. Then make a plan, involve others in your plan, and make it happen!

The Place
Obviously it's normal to think this problem issue is in your church. If it is, then work there. If the stress issue is in your community, or beyond your community, then be creative and find a way through the problem to a solution!

The Price
This one will definitely cost you some time, creativity, teamwork and heart! But money? Most of these kinds of problems can be addressed without much, if any money.

57. Give 'em a Standing "O"!

The Purpose
Even if it's a little embarrassing, we all need some pats on the back or personal recognition from time to time. Your pastor needs to know this too, not just in his head but in his heart. Give him an "O"!

The Plan
Get the word out that everyone is to gather in one location, and then when the pastor enters, everyone goes crazy with applause and cheers! On your feet, foot stompin', hand clappin', hooting and hollering should commence! Add party favors to the mix if you can!

The Place
You can do this with your church staff, with a small group at your church or as a part of your regular worship experience. Yes, we all know that we worship Jesus. This is not about worship. This is about honoring someone that Jesus has used to shepherd you. It's more than OK to do this, it's awesome!

The Price
Obviously it costs NOTHING to give someone a standing ovation. It will take a little time to get the word out, plan the big moment and pull it off. So get started!

58. Put Me in Coach

The Purpose
With the stresses of ministry and the intensity of their calling, members of your pastoral staff may not take the time they should to relax and have fun. Give them an easy way to do it but inviting them to participate with you in sporting activities.

The Plan
It doesn't matter what you pick to do, but its best if you can find something you think your pastor will enjoy. It doesn't have to be a team sport either. Church league softball is nice, but so is a nice relaxing float down the river in a canoe. Be creative.

The Place
This will vary greatly base on what you decide to do. Why not brainstorm a short list of fun sporting activities, and then secretly ask his spouse which one she thinks he would enjoy the most? SKYDIVING? Jump at the chance! GOLF? Join the Club! BOWLING? You can SPARE the time!!

The Price
Many sporting activities are totally free, but some can be quite expensive. Choose what you can afford, and choose what will show your pastor just how much you care!

59. Sticky Notes

The Purpose
It's the little things in life that can mean so much! When your pastor begins to find little Post It notes of affirmation, you'll brighten his day!

The Plan
Be creative in the things you say. Compliment his character, his personality, his talents or some way he has enriched your life and spiritual growth. Wait until you can place the note so that it will be a surprise.

The Place
There are so many options when deciding where to post your sticky notes. You could stick one to his computer monitor. You could post one on the podium in the church, so he sees it when he comes to preach on Sunday. You could even post one on his rearview mirror of his car if he leaves it unlocked!

The Price
Post-It notes are so inexpensive you do this for nearly nothing! Want to have even more fun with this? Invite 100 of your closest friends to do it with you!

60. Love Boxer

The Purpose
Who doesn't love to open a gift? Better yet, who doesn't love to be told they are loved? Why not do both for your pastor? Give a gift of love that he will never forget!

The Plan
Enlist all of the staff at your church, key leaders and anyone else who will join in to write a short note to the pastor, telling him what they love most about him, and one special wish or blessing that want for his life. Gather up the notes, put them in a gift box, wrap it up and present it to your pastor. If you want to make it extra special, send word back to other churches where your pastor has served, and see if they will promote this at their church, inviting notes to be sent from them as well!

The Place
This is a great gift to give at a special anniversary of tenure for your pastor (his 5, 10 or 20 year celebration of ministry or time at your church). Make sure everyone who writes a note is aware of when the presentation will be made!

The Price
Except for a box and a little gift wrap paper, this gift shouldn't cost you anything but some time!

APPETIZERS ARE IN ORDER- INEXPENSIVE IDEAS

61. Float Some Java

The Purpose
Nearly everyone enjoys a great cup of Joe. Rather than having your pastor drink that bargain brand in the 10 pound canister that came from the warehouse store, why not get him some of the good stuff?

The Plan
Consider these options. Sign him up for a "Coffee of the Month" club, and have it delivered to his house. Another choice would be to go to your local Starbucks or coffee store and buy him unique and freshly ground coffee and drop it off yourself. If he has a Keurig, find out his favorite brand, and buy him several boxes of cups!

The Place
The best place to give or send this coffee is to his house. It will encourage him to sit and relax at home before coming to the office. Remind him of that in a note accompanying the coffee!

The Price
Look for bargains and you can find them! This can be a onetime deal, or a once a month deal… and that will affect how expensive it is. Want to spread out the cost? Invite several friends to dive in on this project with you!

62. Discount Dining

The Purpose
Sometimes it's just nice after a long day at work to eat dinner without having to cook or clean it up. The same goes for those that lead our churches! Give your pastor and his family a night at their favorite restaurant

The Plan
Be as sneaky as you need to be to discover what their favorite family restaurant is. Pick up one or more gift certificates for them to enjoy!

The Place
Make sure the place you pick is one they do enjoy, or will enjoy. A gift certificate to a Sushi restaurant may be something you love, but if they don't care for sushi, then it's a wasted effort!

The Price
If you have several families that want to join in on this project, the cost can be very small for everyone involved! Make the calls, get others on board with the plan, and make it happen!

63. I Had the Time of My Life

The Purpose
Whether you know it or not, your pastor may have always wanted to take a dance class… or see a rock concert… or go trout fishing. Find out what his bucket list items are, and see if you can make one of them happen.

The Plan
If you don't know what things are on your pastors' bucket list, the easy way to find out is to ask him. Be sneaky though… bring up "bucket lists" in conversation, share some of your own items, and then ask what his are. Pick one that you can afford and that you can make happen, and then go for it.

The Place
You may not be able to actually be there when this gift takes place, but that's ok! The main point is that your pastor will be able to be there, and that's what counts!

The Price
There are tons of things your pastor may want to experience, see or do that cost absolutely nothing, or very little. Focus on those here. It really is the thought that counts!

64. Feed the Soul

The Purpose
Pastors have a dangerous tendency to study and read so they can teach someone else, but not for their own personal growth. You can help your pastor focus on his own needs.

The Plan
Your other pastoral staff, secretarial staff or his spouse will probably know what books, periodicals or music he has been wanting to add to his library. Find out from them, and then buy it for him. If you're still uncertain what he might want, then buy a gift certificate to your local bookstore or to Amazon.com.

The Place
Wrap up your gift with a loving but stern note. Let him know you expect him to do more than lead your church to grow spiritually. You expect him to grow spiritually, and to feed his own soul as well!

The Price
Books, periodicals and music can be purchased very inexpensively. Everything gets cheaper when more people are involved, so consider doing this as a small group project, or a group of age level workers.

65. Best Meal of the Day

The Purpose
Help your pastoral staff to get a head start on a great day with a healthy breakfast! Have them skip their normal donut and Dr. Pepper routine in favor of a hearty breakfast buffet!

The Plan
Enlist some volunteers to meet with you early one morning at your church. Prepare a health breakfast buffet, including fruit, an omelet bar, and of course lots and lots of bacon (it doesn't have to ALL be healthy)!

The Place
Do this at your church, but be sure and give your staff advance warning so that they won't eat breakfast before coming to work, and that they will make sure their schedule is clear to relax and enjoy this breakfast blessing!

The Price
Supplies for this event will be the only cost. Build your team of volunteers, then build your menu. You may have some volunteers that have a breakfast item specialty they want to contribute, and they may cover the cost for their item.

66. Relaxable

The Purpose
Tension. It's just a natural part of ministry. Stress has a way of building up in the heart and the shoulder muscles of your pastoral staff. Hire a massage therapist as a part of a "Take a Chill Pill" day for your pastoral staff!

The Plan
Hire a massage therapist to come to your church for an hour or two. They can set up in the main office so there isn't a hint of impropriety. If you don't think this is a good idea, then spring for a gift certificate for a 30 minute massage.

The Place
The great thing about doing this at the church office is that one therapist could give a 10 to 15 minute shoulder and neck massage to several of your pastoral staff members in a couple of hours' time.

The Price
You can hire a massage therapist to come to your church office for a couple of hours, and it won't cost you an arm or a leg.

67. Random is Good

The Purpose
Random surprises... it's incredibly fun to give them, and even more fun to receive them! Surprise your pastoral staff with some random gifts!

The Plan
These gifts don't really have to make sense. A Butterfinger bar, movie tickets, gift cards, beef jerky, flowers, a Mr. Potato Head... all are fun and random gifts that are sure to make your pastor smile! They are especially fun if you can leave a message with a meaning with your gift. For instance, with movie tickets you might say, "You're one of my heroes! Now go watch your favorite superhero at the movies!"

The Place
You can leave the random gift in your pastors' office, the front seat of his car, send it in the mail, or have it delivered by a singing telegram. Just be random!

The Price
Tons of fun and random gifts can be had for little or no charge! Just don't steal the yard gnome from the yard of your neighbor and give it to your pastor. That could cause a problem.

68. Scrapbooking

The Purpose
Your pastor is worth remembering. His ministry, his family and his life make a difference. Gather together the pictures, news articles or other memorable clips and put together a scrapbook.

The Plan
You can gather pics that other church members have taken, ask for pictures from his family and other staff, or plan this scrapbook for NEXT year, and intentionally shoot pictures all year long for the scrapbook you will create! Be sure if you borrow pictures that you get the originals back to their owner!

The Place
There are tons of supplies you can purchase to create your own home made scrapbook from stores like Wal-Mart or Target, or you can scan your pictures and have a website like www.scrapbook.com, www.shutterfly.com or www.smilebox.com create one for you!

The Price
If you create a scrapbook yourself, you can do it for under $20. If you choose to have one created professionally online, it could cost anywhere from $15 to $150. Choose what fits your timeline and budget best!

69. Snacktacular

The Purpose
Don't we all have a favorite snack? Does your past love Cheetos, Snickers or frozen grapes the most? Do you even know? Well go find out and feed his snack need!

The Plan
When the snack monster attacks our appetite, we tend to reach for anything close! It's even better if what is close is the snack we love the most! Stock up and build a Snack Basket for your pastor for those times between meals when those cravings hit!

The Place
Once you have your basket of his favorite snacks put together, present it as a gift of your appreciation and love for all he does for your church! This is a cool event to do for all of your pastoral staff at once!

The Price
You can buy baskets cheap at the Dollar Store, and snacks aren't really that expensive either! Enlist a different person to put together the Snack Basket for each of your pastoral staff and minimize the cost by spreading out the expense among several people!

70. Drinks are on the House

The Purpose
Your pastor most likely has the whole "living water" thing covered in his life. It's his love for Diet Coke, bottled water or Orange Crush that needs some help! Feed the need!

The Plan
You probably already know what the favorite drink of your pastor is, since he mostly like has one with him much of the time! Check out where your purchase his favorite drink in bulk, and surprise him with a six pack or a case of his most loved liquid!

The Place
Drop his beverage gift off at the church office, wrapped up in a bow with a card telling him you appreciate him! If you can make a play on words, it's even better (i.e., "You CRUSHed that sermon on Sunday", or "You're just what the DR. ordered")

The Price
A few bucks for a six pack is not much to pay to make his day! A case isn't really that much more, and goes a long way to making many more of his days happy!

71. Employee of the Month/Year

The Purpose
Yes, companies still do this, so why not your church?! You can choose a "Pastor of the Month!", or "Pastor of the Year!", and provide some fun and special perks to go with the title to show your appreciation.

The Plan
Brainstorm a list of ideas to show your appreciation. They might include a reserved parking space for him or his spouse, a weekend off or dinner out with his spouse and/or his family. Then pass the list on to your Personnel Team at the church, or whatever group within your church that has the authority to make this happen!

The Place
Promote this event through your church newsletter or Sunday Bulletin and make sure everyone knows about it. Invite them to come up with their own gift or token of appreciation!

The Price
Many of the best perks you could offer are free, but don't be afraid to turn loose with a little cash as icing on the "You're Really Special" cake!

72. Gag Them

The Purpose
Don't you just love a great gag gift!? My guess is that your pastor will too! Find a funny gift to lift his spirits for the day!

The Plan
Unleash your creativity here! Buy him a talking "Billy Bass", a subscription to a crazy magazine, or a referee stress doll that has arms, legs and head that are attached by Velcro, so they can be torn off and put back together while they watch their favorite sporting event! None of these appeal to you? Simply go to Google and type in "Gag gifts", and I'm sure you'll find something that would be the perfect gag gift!

The Place
A great place to present your gag gift would be during a drop by visit to the weekly staff meeting! The other pastors will enjoy the fun, and you can build anticipation if you take turns presenting your gift to the different staff pastors!

The Price
These gifts don't have to be expensive to make a big splash! Just be tasteful, fun and remember that we all like to be laughed with but not laughed at! Gag gifts should make the receiver of the gift laugh as much as those who are giving the gift, or watching it be given.

73. Filler Up

The Purpose
Of all the money we have to spend on the necessities of life, I have yet to find anyone who enjoys spending money at the gas pump. So pick up the tab for a gas gift card, or even for filling up the entire gas tank for your pastor!

The Plan
Many gas stations now offer gift cards, so it's easy to pick one up, drop it in a nice card with a personalized note, and hand it off to him after church or at the church office.

The Place
Make sure that if your pastor has a preference about where he buys his fuel that you purchase your gift card at that location. You can just as easily stop by his office and ask him to follow you to the gas station, fill his car up, and then pay for it.

The Price
You can spend $10 or $20 on a gas card, or you might choose to fill up the entire tank! Do whatever your checking account can handle!

74. DJ Pastor

The Purpose
Slapping on a set of headphones and enjoying some tunes is a great way for your pastor to unwind a little. Music is an incredible stress reliever and source of pleasure. Give the gift of music to your pastor and watch the smiles begin!

The Plan
So much of music sales today s through a digital format, so be careful before you spend money here. You can buy a CD, and then they could copy that to their computer/phone/MP3 player. You may choose to skip that step, and if your pastor uses iTunes or another music service you can buy a gift card so he can choose his own music.

The Place
Drop your CD or music gift card in his hand in the hall before church begins. It's amazing how being blessed by one of your church members can add a little extra zip to the spirit of your pastor right before he leads your church in worship or preaching!

The Price
Plan to spend from $10 or more on music. Individual songs purchased online run from .69 for oldies, on up to $1.29 or more for current hits. Buy more than one song. That would be weird to just by one song.

75. Reading All Year Long

The Purpose
Hobbies are a great way for your pastor to unwind, stay fresh and invest in his own sanity! Whatever their hobbies or interests are, find a way to show your appreciation for him by supporting his hobby interests!

The Plan
Work with his spouse or the other pastoral staff members to discover what his hobbies or special interests are. If you already know, then you're halfway to success! Once you know what it is, order them a printed or a digital subscription that speaks to their hobby or interest.

The Place
Have the subscription sent to their home, but announce the gift with a card and an appreciative note from you. You don't want your pastor to think the subscription is a mistake and try to cancel it or pay for it!

The Price
These kinds of subscriptions can be anywhere from $10 to over $100 annually, so shop around for a deal and check out a variety of options! If you order it through Publishers Clearing House, you too might become a winner!

76. Gift Basket of the Month

The Purpose
Getting a special seasonal gift as a token of appreciation is a wonderful gesture! What could be better?? How about a different season gift several times throughout the year!

The Plan
Be intentional, be creative and communicate the surprise! Think through the year, and plan a "Winter Nights", "Spring Has Sprung", "Summertime Fun" and "Fall Festival" basket! Fill each basket with goodies that somehow symbolize the season, or help your pastor enjoy the season more. Let him know to expect the baskets- this will help build some anticipation and excitement leading up to each new surprise!

The Place
Present the baskets over dinner, beside the pool or on a picnic... just have fun building up the surprise, including the location and timing of the gift!

The Price
Depending on whether you fill the basket with homemade goodies, inexpensive trinkets or gift certificates for special nights out, the price on this activity can range from FREE to moderately expensive! Just don't be boring, make the building of the basket an exercise in creativity and fun!

77. Mouse on the Face

The Purpose
Your pastor probably spends a fair amount of time working at their computer. Preparing Bible studies, sending emails or doing research, computer time can pile up. Bring the joy of seeing an image on their mousepad that will brighten their day!

The Plan
There are plenty of websites on the internet that will allow you upload your picture of one of their loved ones, their favorite sports team logo or entertainment icon and have it printed on a mousepad.

The Place
Websites like www.visitaprint.com, www.shutterfly.com or www.zazzle.com are only a few of those on the internet that will produce a custom mousepad to your specifications!

The Price
Cost on these custom mousepads is very inexpensive! You can find mousepads with your custom uploaded picture imprinted on them in prices ranging from $10 to $20, with shipping cost included!

78. My Other Shirt is a Collar

The Purpose
Your pastor wants desperately to be the best shepherd you've ever had. His heart is to lead, disciple and pastor with excellence! Why not help him tell other people what you already know?!

The Plan
With t-shirt technology advancing every day, it's easy to have a custom screened shirt for very little money. You can provide the words and digital graphics to a local t-shirt company, or an online distributor and create the perfect shirt as a gift for your pastor! "Best Pastor in (your city)", "My other shirt is a collar!", or "My church thinks I'm the bomb diggity!" are just a few ideas

The Place
Check out your local t-shirt distributor first, but if you don't have one, or just want to check out your other options, look at www.customink.com, www.imprint.com or www.uberprints.com for a variety of colors, styles and options!

The Price
Custom shirts can range from $10 to $25 apiece, depending on the designs, quality of shirt and type of shirt you're designing. Make it something he'll be proud to wear for years to come!

79. Flip Flopper

The Purpose
So much stress, pressure and work are a natural part of ministry that sometimes it's hard for your pastor to remember that he needs to relax every now and then! Help him "flip" that workaholic attitude, and "flop" into some relaxing shoes!

The Plan
Be sure you find out what his correct shoe size is, or this gift really will be a flop! With an accurate shoe size in hand, make your way to the shoe store or department store and buy him a set of trendy flip flops. (Yes, some people call them 'thongs', but if you're not careful here you might have the salesperson bring you the wrong item!)

The Place
This is a great gift to pass out to your pastoral staff at their staff meeting! Let them know how much you appreciate all they do, but remind them that they are best able to take care of the church when they have taken good care of themselves, and that means taking some time to relax & refresh!

The Price
Flip flops are fairly inexpensive, ranging in cost from $6 to $26, depending on the brand, the logo and the quality of the shoe. If they are cheap enough, pick him up a couple of different styles and colors of shoes.

80. Cookies & Fruit & Stuff Oh My

The Purpose
Pastors love to eat! Cookie bouquet? Yes please! Edible Arrangement of fruit? Of course! Store bought, homemade or internet ordered? Who cares, it's all YUMMY!

The Plan
If you have the time and ability to create one of these food masterpieces, by all means go for it! Decorate the cookies or dip the fruit in chocolate and nuts, or buy the fresh fruit and create a unique display (Noah's Ark from a carved watermelon, with little fruit animals?) Make it delicious and make it memorable!

The Place
If your gifts are not culinary in nature, then maybe you'll opt to swing by the local bakery and order a cookie or cupcake "cake", or hop on the internet and order something sweet from www.berries.com or www.ediblearrangements.com. They have huge assortments of predesigned gifts, or create your own surprise combo!

The Price
If you are creating your own special surprise, you can usually do this for under $20! If you plan on ordering a special sweetness to be delivered by one of the online merchants, you can expect to spend anywhere from $30 to $100.

81. Marshmallows or Whipped

The Purpose
Coffee… the nectar that rejuvenates our spirits, calms our jitters (for a moment, anyway!) and allows us to talk intelligently to others at the beginning of the day! Make your pastor's day by bringing him his favorite!

The Plan
Although some gift ideas should be surprises, give your pastor a heads up the day before that you'll be dropping off a special coffee surprise the next day! That way he won't beat you to punch and stop off and get his own! Ask if he has a favorite flavor and toppings, and make sure you make it happen!

The Place
If your pastor has a local spot that has his favorite, then by all means stop there to get the stuff that keeps his morning chugging on! For a fun time, why not consider inviting all of the pastoral staff to just stop off at the local coffee watering hole together, and then you pick up the tab!

The Price
A cup of Joe is a little more expensive than it used to be. McDonalds has good coffee cheap, and Starbucks can tap you for $4 to $8 per cup. You decide!

82. Seeing the Silver Screen

The Purpose
The competition to produce quality movies is at a fever pitch in our society. Sometimes your pastor could really use the mindless pleasure of watching a car chase, space invader or chick flick. Give him the gift of a movie!

The Plan
This works great if you can arrange for the pastor and/or the staff to take some time off in the afternoon to watch the movie. Matinee prices are usually cheaper too! Give them a couple of weeks' notice so that they don't go see the movie on their own, but can enjoy the group experience!

The Place
You may be limited with movie locations, but if you're close to a movie theater that has the "lounge chair" seating, or a private screening room where you could provide snacks, that would just be the icing on the cake for this event!

The Price
Movie tickets can cost between $6 for a matinee to $12 apiece. Factor in cost for popcorn, snacks and drinks too! There's nothing goes together like exploding cars & Raisinets, or movie villains & hot buttered popcorn!

83. Thirsty?

The Purpose
It's a pretty good bet that your pastor has a favorite beverage… sweet tea from Sonic Drive-In, ice cold Dr. Pepper or a caramel macchiato frappe something from down the street! Be his hero and drop one off as a surprise!

The Plan
Touch base with his spouse to discover his concoction of choice, and then make sure with his secretary or someone at the church that he is going to be in the office. It's a huge fail as a gift if he's not there to receive it!

The Place
Before you pick up his drink, stop off and pick up a humorous card, and write a note telling him what you appreciate the most about his heart! Then hand card and drink to him and pop out of his office as quickly as you popped in!

The Price
This gift is a very inexpensive way to show your appreciation! It really isn't the cost of the gift that matters, but the thoughtfulness and the time you took that will let him know how much he is loved and appreciated.

84. Flexible is the New YES!

The Purpose
People are unique. Some are morning people, others are night owls. Seasons of life cause our needs to vary as well. Pastors with young children obviously have different needs than empty nesters. What if your church recognized these differences and worked with your staff to build work schedules that recognized and accounted for those differences?

The Plan
This item takes a lot of communication and coordination between your staff, church leadership and Personnel Team. Pastors will need to have times that they are all present and working together. Pastors also need to be available to church members at times that are convenient to them as well. But with some work and finesse, this can be one of the coolest things you can do for your staff.

The Place
Another option in this puzzle might be to consider allowing members of your staff to spend some of their work/study schedule working from their home office, or at the local Starbucks/bookstore/library.

The Price
There isn't any real expense in making this happen, except for the time and coordination that it takes to make sure everyone is communicating well and that all of the important tasks and ministries are being handled well.

85. Say it with Flowers

The Purpose
Nothing brightens a desk or a day like getting flowers! The look beautiful, they smell fantastic, but most of all they shout to the recipient "I think you're wonderful!" Don't think this is only a gift that women appreciate either, because guys love flowers too!

The Plan
You can order flowers to have them delivered, pick some up from the floral department of your local grocery store, or cut some fresh from your own garden and deliver them yourself!

The Place
This is a great gift to send to their office for lots of reasons. It's typically the place they spend the majority of their time, so they will get the most pleasure out of them if they are at the office. It also sends a message to everyone that comes by their office that it's a good thing to show appreciation to the pastoral staff!

The Price
The cost here runs from FREE if you grow, cut and deliver the flowers yourself, around $25-$50 if you pick some up at the grocery store, and upwards to $100 if you order from the florist and have it delivered. Do what works best for your budget.

86. Proclamation & Seal

The Purpose
Who doesn't like to feel like they are very, very special?! You can issue your own "Greatest Pastor in the World" proclamation and present it to your pastor to let him know just what they mean to you and your church!

The Plan
There are tons of different software programs that you can use to create your "proclamation" certificate- Word, Publisher, Photoshop, just to name a few. Make the language pompous and flowery. If you aren't sure what to say, then search the internet for examples and customize to your pastor. This certificate looks really cool if you purchase a gold seal sticker and have a notary press it with their seal!

The Place
Why not make this presentation to your pastor or entire staff as a surprise one Sunday morning as the service begins?! This allows everyone to be in on this presentation and give a rousing round of applause to affirm the staff!

The Price
You can pick up parchment paper and gold seals for very little expense, usually under $20. If you really want to do it right, frame it too, but that does add to the cost for each presentation about $10.

87. Put Their Mug on a Mug

The Purpose
Personalized mugs are a cute and fun way to let your pastoral staff know that you appreciate their mugshot, so you put it on a mug!

The Plan
Don't just settle for a boring head shot of your pastor for this mug! Get a funny picture, a silly selfie or a picture him with you or others in the church. The goal is to make him smile every time he looks at that mug, so let that be your guiding factor in choosing the picture.

The Place
You may have local vendors who can do this, but if not then head to the internet. Check out www.vistaprint.com, www.shutterfly.com or even www.walgreens.com to upload your digital pic and order your mug!

The Price
Mugs like this vary greatly in cost, running from $10 to $50 each, so shop around and get the best buy! For and extra fun twist, why not order a custom mug for each member of the pastor's family, with a funny picture of each family member on their own mug?!

88. Gratitude Journal

The Purpose
Pastors, more than anything else, want to honor God with their service. What's almost as important is feeling like their efforts are genuinely making a positive impact on the lives of those they serve. By keeping a journal of the things your pastor has taught you, and then sharing that with him could mean the world to his ministry.

The Plan
Buy a blank journal, and then for one year, look for those teachable moments in life, in sermons and in conversation with your pastor where he taught you something. Record those things you learned in the journal, and record them in a conversational tone, as if you were visiting with your pastor. At the end of one year, present that journal to him as a gift.

The Place
This is a gift best given in a small group. Maybe you can convince a few others to do this at the same time, and you can hold each other accountable to stay up with it. Then meet with your pastor as a group and present your journals to him.

The Price
The cost of the journal is low, roughly $10 to $20. But it's your time and dedication to learning and to sharing what you've learned with your pastor that will mean the most.

89. Treat Them like Royalty

The Purpose
Your pastoral staff truly are servants in your church, but never forget that they are also children of the King! Why not pass this honor around your staff, and make them "king" or "queen" for the week!

The Plan
You can pick up a fun crown at a party supply store, and maybe even a scepter too! As royalty for the day, they get primo parking privileges, lunch brought to their desk or a free lunch at the restaurant. Best of all, they get to take the afternoon off to spend with the "royal family"!

The Place
This could be a practice that takes place once per quarter, and happens during a staff meeting! Include music, and official proclamation, and a bouquet of their favorite candy or flowers for the coronation! A sign over their office door is a nice touch as well!

The Price
You can easily pull this off for under $25 each time you do it, and you can be as creative and fun with it as you want to!

90. Dropping Off Lunch

The Purpose
It's the thought that counts, but food is really, really good too! If you know that your pastor is going to be working hard on a project or event, then why not swing by the church with his favorite lunch in a sack to give him the boost and the Kudos he deserves!?

The Plan
Make sure that if you're going to do this, that you cover a few bases. First, make sure the food you bring is something he likes, and something he didn't just eat yesterday. Next, be early, in case he actually did decide he was going to try to get out for lunch. Finally, if you have the time, take your own lunch too, and ask if he'd like company!

The Place
Call ahead and make sure he's aware that you're dropping lunch off, and then be prompt- and prompt is 10 minutes early!

The Price
This could be the best $10 you've ever spent, just bringing your lunch and your friendship to the table! Enjoy!

91. Mighty Morphing Trophy

The Purpose
Trophies rock! Customized trophies are even better! This traveling trophy award has a unique spin on it, because the trophy changes and gets more awesome over time!

The Plan
Get a big trophy… as big as you can find. Usually someone has an old one in their garage or attic just gathering dust. Remove the nameplate and have a new one made that says, "Awesome Staff Award!". It can be presented to a different staff member weekly, quarterly or annually, whichever works best. The trick is, each time it is presented, the current recipient needs to find a small item that they think best represents the character or a quality of the next recipient, and then glues or otherwise attaches that to the trophy! It truly is a new trophy every time it is presented!

The Place
This is a really fun staff meeting event. Someone outside of the church staff can make the choice as to who the recipient is, but the presentation could be made during the staff meeting by the previous recipient.

The Price
Old trophies are free, and each recipient donates their own new item to the trophy, so the only real cost here is the new nameplate, which should be under $10.

92. Plaque Treatment

The Purpose
Although similar to the "Mighty Morphing Trophy", this is a little more serious. You can name a process or an award after a pastoral staff member, or name it after a lay person that everyone respects. The award can represent a special character trait or spiritual quality.

The Plan
Use this as a time to reinforce those key qualities or behaviors that you want your staff to excel in. Have nice plaque made at a trophy shop, with a place for name plates at the bottom. That way each year you can add a plate with the name, year and character trait you're recognizing. Another twist on this might be to name a room, process or event after someone.

The Place
Present this award annually at the staff Christmas party. Although you love to encourage all of your staff, awards just aren't that special if everyone gets an award every time.

The Price
A one-time price of about $50 should purchase a nice plaque for this award. Each year after will be a minimal cost to have the new name plate made for the bottom section of the plaque. Have this award posted somewhere in the church office or foyer for all to see.

93. Bring the Midway Home

The Purpose
Walking into a room and having the wave of fresh popped popcorn hit their nose is a great way to say "Hey, we love you!" to your pastoral staff! Popcorn says fun, it says happy and it says have a great day… so do some popcorn!

The Plan
You can rent an old fashioned popcorn popper, or find an organization or church that will loan you one that they have. Show up early, and have the popcorn popped, hot and ready for the staff when they arrive!

The Place
The church office is the best place to do this! Everyone gets to benefit from the hot popcorn, even the folks who may drop by the church during the day.

The Price
Party supply stores will rent these out for $50 to $100 per day, and the cost of the oil, popcorn and butter is very cheap! Spring for a little extra and get the flavored popcorn salt, and fun bags to put the popcorn into!

94. Sabbatical

The Purpose
Sometimes the pressures of living in the ministry "fishbowl" can be overwhelming, both to the pastor and to his family. Some time away to refresh and revitalize their spirits is a super way as a church to affirm your love for them.

The Plan
Work through your Personnel Team or whoever it is at your church that makes decisions regarding benefits and time off. Convince them to establish a "Sabbatical Policy" if they have not already done so. Sabbaticals could vary from 2 weeks to 3 months. Your church might want to have staff go on sabbatical once every 3, 5 or 7 years, whatever you feel is best for their spiritual and relational health.

The Place
Make sure that the policy on sabbaticals requires that there are ZERO ministry expectations on the staff member. This is not supposed to be a time where you send them to a conference or convention. If they choose to go to an event for refreshing and encouragement, that's great, but it shouldn't be an expectation of the church.

The Price
The budget here is wide open. Your church should decide in each case what it wants to make available to your pastoral staff financially during a sabbatical period. Some churches simply give the time off, while others offer to absorb some of the cost. You decide what works best for your church.

95. Making History

The Purpose
You most likely have "scrapbookers" in your church who would love to take the lead on this- it might even be you! Creating a historical scrapbook that chronicles the life and ministry events in your church is a neat way to help your pastoral staff go down in history.

The Plan
Purchase a scrapbook and the necessary supplies to log the activities and events that happen in your church. Build a network of people who will take pictures, gather mementos and other things to put in the scrapbook. You can do a new and fresh book each year, and present last years' book to your staff at the beginning of each New Year.

The Place
This could be the centerpiece of an after church fellowship built around the "Look What God Has Done!" theme. Invited everyone to bring their own pictures and memories to share as well.

The Price
The cost of a nice scrapbook and supplies should be under $50, and the only costs after that are the moments you and others spend in putting it all together.

96. Roll Out the Donuts

The Purpose
Donuts… everyone's best breakfast buddy! Many of your pastors are in such a rush to get out the door and to work that they neglect eating breakfast. Spoil them with their favorite donut, bear claw or long john!

The Plan
Swing by the donut shop and order a variety of pastries, enough for each person in the church office to have a couple. That will give them one in the morning, and then when that sugar high wears off after lunch, they can get another fix to carry them until closing time!

The Place
Drop the donuts off at the church office, and make sure that you gave them a one day warning. It spoils the fun if they stopped off somewhere on the way to the church and bought their own donuts!

The Price
Donuts and juice/milk for each person can be done for around $3 per person, so it's cheap enough to include everyone in the office! Remember, make it special, and if you can, get some of the donuts with sprinkles!

97. Wall of Famer

The Purpose
No matter the size of your church, big or small, it's always nice to give people a way to get to know your pastoral staff better. Don't take for granted that everyone knows the pastors and their families. This "Wall of Fame" is a simple but effective way to strengthen the familiarity and friendship between your staff and the church.

The Plan
Collect several fun pictures of your staff and their families, and then write up a brief bio for them. Frame the pictures and the bio together and place them on display. Be sure and use the church bulletin or newsletter to promote this so that people will know to go check it out.

The Place
Create your "Wall of Fame" of your church staff in the church foyer, Fellowship Hall or other public location. For an added touch, put notecards and a drop box near this display for church members to write a brief note to the staff letting them know how much they are appreciated.

The Price
This will cost you some time, elbow grease and maybe $15 per frame for the pictures and bio sheet... an incredible bargain for the benefit!

98. Slinging Web Stuff

The Purpose
Are you a tech person, or do you know someone that is? What if you used those abilities to create a fun website dedicated to honoring your pastoral staff!?

The Plan
Web domains are cheap, and building/maintaining a website has become a very easy process, even for someone with limited technical abilities. To build this website, you'll want to keep it updated and current, with new pictures and commentary, and especially links to the email addresses of your pastoral staff, so people can quickly shoot them an email of affirmation!

The Place
Choose a fun web domain, and use a service like www.register.com, www.domain.com or www.namecheap.com to search for available website names. Make it something people can easily remember. Don't spoil the surprise... only share the final website when it is completed!

The Price
Web domains can be purchased for $.99 to thousands of dollars, depending on who owns it. Other costs will include web hosting and other associated costs with maintaining the website. This is where you should defer to your technical friends for advice and direction!

99. Stocking Up the Good Stuff

The Purpose
Bring a smile to their face when your pastoral staff discovers you've stocked the supply room or conference room at the church with flavored creamers, juice, pop or other snacks!

The Plan
The easiest way to do this is to go the grocery store and just buy what you think they would like to munch on. A little more work might yield a better result though. Consider surveying your staff about what their favorite drinks, snacks, coffees, etc. are, and they purchasing those items that fit their own unique tastes!

The Place
This is intended to be a special treat for your staff to enjoy on an ongoing basis, NOT for them to enjoy one week, and then have it scavenged bare by church members the next Sunday. Put these supplies somewhere they can be secured and kept for the enjoyment of the staff.

The Price
You can do a great job of stocking up goodies for between $50 & $100. Do the right thing… don't buy generic because it's cheaper! Buy the good stuff!

Belly Up for the Main Course! This May Cost a Little

100. Smells Like Team Spirit

The Purpose
Pastors avoid the appearance of "favorites" when it comes to working with other staff or with church members. They do, however, have their favorite sports teams, rock stars and other heroes! Why not by them a jersey or a shirt recognizing their team spirit!

The Plan
Usually there's not a lot of effort that has to go into discovering their favorite college or pro sports team, or other favorite performer. Still, it's important that you clarify that with their spouse or someone else on church staff to make sure. Then try to purchase a shirt or jersey that identifies that loyalty, either at a sporting goods store or on the internet. Also double check the size to make sure you purchase something that fits!

The Place
Places like Academy Sports, Hibbet's, Dick's Sporting Goods or even department stores like Wal-Mart or Target carry a huge selection of jerseys. If you can't find what you like in a store, hop onto the internet and you're sure to find a great deal that perfectly fits your needs!

The Price
Shirts or jerseys can cost anywhere from $15 to $150 dollars, depending on what you're looking for, and the quality of the clothing. Purchasing things on the internet will also usually have shipping charges too, so don't forget to factor that cost in as well.

101. Brand Them

The Purpose
One unique way to set your pastoral staff apart and honor their service is to have a special piece of clothing- shirt, jacket or ball cap- monogrammed with the church logo!

The Plan
Be sure and get the right sizes for everyone on the church pastoral staff. This gift needs to fit! Order everyone the same color, and have the logo monogrammed by a professional. If your church doesn't have a log, simply have the name of the church monogrammed.

The Place
Present the special branded clothing to your pastoral staff during a luncheon, staff party or special service to recognize the service and ministry of your pastoral staff. Have them try it on, and take a group picture for the church newsletter or website!

The Price
You'll want to purchase quality clothing, no matter what you decide to order. Remember, this clothing will not only honor your pastoral staff, but it will be a walking billboard for your church. You'll want it to look nice for a long time, so take your time, spend the money and order the best!

102. Dinner with Leadership

The Purpose
Not everything needs to be an "all church" event. You may choose to do some more intimate relationship with key leadership and your pastoral staff, and a special night out on the town can be an opportunity to build life-long relationships

The Plan
Plan this event far enough in advance that you are certain that your key lay leadership and pastoral staff are all able to attend. It's critical that you make reservations, and that you use a location that allows for some privacy.

The Place
If building relationships, deep conversation and sharing dreams for the future are the focus of this kind of dinner, then a fast food joint busy and loud restaurant are not the optimal locations for you. In some instances, this event can be held in a private home. Whether it happens in a home or in a private room in a nice restaurant, make it a night to remember.

The Price
You may have a church member that is willing to cover the cost for this event, and if so, that's great! In other instances, it may take the coordinated funds of several people to pay for the evening. But no matter what, make sure that the pastoral staff doesn't pay for a thing!

103. You So Fancy

The Purpose
Rather than a group of people gathering for dinner with all of the staff, this event is designed to show one of your pastoral staff a night on the town that he might not otherwise be able to afford or experience on his own! Spoil him and his spouse rotten!

The Plan
Make this a "dress up and get all fancy" kind of night! Let your pastor and his wife know ahead of time where you will be going to eat, and that you will be their guest for the evening!

The Place
Pick someplace that has a great atmosphere, high quality food, and whatever you do, don't skimp out on the appetizers or the desserts! Remember, this event is supposed to be something that overwhelms them, and totally convinces them how much they are loved and appreciated.

The Price
This special thank you dinner may not be for everyone to attempt. However, if God has blessed you in such a way that you can afford a night on the town like this with your pastor and his wife, then go for it!

104. Taking Care of Business

The Purpose
Pastors spend most of their lives planning and working for the benefit of others. Sometimes, without meaning to they can shortchange their own family finances. This might be not managing their funds well in the short-term, or failing to invest for their long term needs like college for the kids or retirement for themselves. You can help them do both.

The Plan
Talk to your pastor first, and with his permission schedule financial planning sessions with a family financial consultant for your pastor and spouse. The consultant can help them get a handle on their current financial situation, and set in place a long-term strategy that will provide for education, vacation and retirement needs in the future!

The Place
Some of your pastor's compensation may be public knowledge through printed budgets and business meetings. However, this session is private, and probably ought to take place at the office of the financial consultant.

The Price
Financial consultants sometimes charge a fee for this kind of counseling, while others make their living off of products they sell or fees for services managing retirement funds. Financial consultants who charge for this service can be fairly expensive, especially if the financial counseling is ongoing over a period of time.

105. Showers of Cards

The Purpose
Give your pastor some special nights out to their favorite restaurant, a shopping spree at the favorite sporting goods or electronics store. How do you make this happen without the hassle of scheduling a time for you to do all of this with him? Gift cards, that's how!

The Plan
Engaging a small group or involving the entire church in this project are great ways to pull this one off! If you have a way to build a "wish list" of the favorite restaurants or stores your pastor loves, it's a helpful way to help your group buy gift cards they can be sure that he will enjoy.

The Place
Invite people to buy gift cards for a "shower of cards" fellowship one evening. Make a special presentation of the cards in a basket, hung on a "card tree" or whatever creative display you can come up with.

The Price
Recommend that people buy a card or cards of varying denominations. They can be $5 to $100 in value. You might also suggest that some of their gift cards be designated for the pastor's spouse and children, to make them feel special and loved.

106. Sacking Groceries

The Purpose
Spending money on vacation is fun! Buying gifts for people we love is exciting! But normal stuff like paying the bills and buying groceries- no one really enjoys that! Why not surprise your pastor by picking up the grocery tab for their family?!

The Plan
There are a couple of ways you can do this. First and most easy would be for you to buy a gift card to the local grocery store, and allow them to use it the next time they go shopping. Another option would be to write them a check or hand them cash in an envelope with the word "GROCERIES" labeled on the outside. Finally, if you're really brave, offer to go grocery shopping with him or his spouse, and at the register, simply step in front of them and pay the bill!

The Place
People can be particular about the brands and types of food they feed their family. Since that may be the case, it's best if you make this happen at the grocery store they are accustomed to using.

The Price
Decide whether you want to set a limit ($100, $200, or more), or if you simply want to buy the groceries they would normally purchase, no matter what the cost.

107. Bobble Head Pastor

The Purpose
Memorialize your pastor with his own "mini me" statue! He will flip when you hand him a customized Bobblehead with his likeness on the noggin!

The Plan
There are a number of websites where you can order a customized bobble head of your pastor. You'll need a high quality headshot picture for the artists who will craft his head to use as a template. Most of these websites will also allow you to choose a customized costume or accessories to go along with your Bobblehead. Pick something that is unique to your pastor. If he's a fisherman, see if they can create him with a little miniature fishing pole. If he loves sports, then create him wearing the uniform of his favorite team!

The Place
Among the websites were you can order your custom Bobblehead are www.bobbleheads.com, www.bobblemaker.com, www.1minime.com or www.likenessme.com.

The Price
When ordering a Bobblehead, you might spend anywhere from $75 to $200. These creations take time, so be sure to give yourself plenty of time to have your creation made.

108. Maid in America

The Purpose
Everyone loves posh treatment at one time or another. Spoil your pastor and his family by providing maid service for them, and giving their house an incredible cleaning from top to bottom!

The Plan
Check out different cleaning companies on the internet, using Google references, websites like the Better Business Bureau and www.angieslist.com, and references from the websites of the cleaning company's own website to make sure you hire a quality company. You'll also want to gather all of this information, and then talk to your pastor and his family about it. Some people might feel awkward about having strangers in their home cleaning. Let your pastor know you've checked them out thoroughly, and that it's a blessing you want to give them!

The Place
You'll want to gift wrap this gift certificate in a fun way- tape it to a duster, or put it in a basket with empty bottles of cleaning supplies!

The Price
Maid services charge anywhere from $25 to $50 per hour. Purchase a plan that will cover cleaning their entire house from top to bottom. It may take anywhere from 3 to 8 hours, so you could spend from $75 to $400, depending on how large your pastor's home is.

109. Personal Assistant for a Day

The Purpose
It seems that for most of us the busyness of our work lives crowds out the time we want to spend on our personal projects and hobbies. By hiring a personal assistant for your pastor for a day, you can help him catch up on so many of his details he will have time left over to spend on the fun stuff!

The Plan
For your pastor to get the most out of this activity, he will need a couple of weeks to plan the schedule, activities, tasks and projects he will want help with, and what he will want the personal assistant to accomplish or work on. Let your pastor know what the skill set of the personal assistant is, and how long they will be available to him.

The Place
Give your pastor a gift certificate in a classy business envelope, informing him of his impending "assistant assignment"!

The Price
The price for a personal assistant will vary greatly based upon their skills and expertise. People with high technical abilities will be more expensive than someone with basic office skills. You should count on 8 hours of work, and plan on spending anywhere from $10 to $30 per hour.

110. Home Improvement

The Purpose
While your pastor might be handy in the pulpit, it doesn't necessarily mean he's a handyman around his own home! Home repairs and maintenance tasks can pile up on the home front, and you could be his handyman to the rescue!

The Plan
Ask your pastor's spouse to come up with a list of handyman projects that desperately need done around their house. Then plan to do what you can to make them happen, whether that means doing them yourself, finding volunteers in your church, or hiring someone professionally to do them. Do NOT do anything halfway! If neither you nor a volunteer can perform the tasks with excellence, then hire a professional.

The Place
Drop by your pastor's home (of course, his spouse is in on the secret) and deliver the list of "honey do's" that need done around the house… and then let him know that you've made arrangements to have them "honey DONE"!

The Price
Some churches are blessed to have lots of handyman professionals, while in other instances the handyman well is dry. You may be able to do this set of tasks for free, but they could cost upwards to a $1,000. But in the words of that great philosopher Larry the Cable guy, "Git R Done"!

111. Flip This Office

The Purpose
Your pastor spends a ton of his time at work in his office. Wouldn't it be nice to do a makeover of his office space that makes it more inviting, comfortable and customized to his personality?

The Plan
It's critical that you involve the proper people before you take on this project. If your church has a properties committee or team in charge of facilities, you'll want to communicate with them, and obtain any necessary permissions, equipment or supplies to make the necessary remodels. You'll also need to get approval from your budget team if you will be spending money for the remodel. Get your pastor's input regarding colors, furniture or floor covering changes!

The Place
If this makeover could take place on a Saturday, it would be less likely to interfere with your pastor and his preparations for Sunday. Move everything out of his office on Friday evening, and make it a one day, super cool makeover!

The Price
Office makeovers can be minimal, with a can of paint and some curtains. But they could also include new floor coverings, furniture and art! Plan on somewhere between $100 and $3,000 in total costs.

112. Don't Muzzle the Ox

The Purpose
There are so many ideas for ways to show your pastor how much you care about him, but one of the very best ways is simply to pay him well!

The Plan
Most churches organize their finances through the use of a budget committee or team. They typically work in conjunction with a personnel team when it comes to recommendations regarding compensation. Prepare for any conversation you might have with these groups by investigating what the total benefit packages are for pastors of churches your size, including retirement, health and pay. Use these as a starting point in developing a recommendation that your staff be compensated well for their service.

The Place
Any recommendations you might have ought to be done respectfully and in writing. The floor of a church business meeting is not an appropriate place or method of encouraging better pay for your pastoral staff. Take the high road and go the extra mile in making intelligent and courteous suggestions regarding pastoral compensation.

The Price
Remember, pastors ought to be compensated fairly based on these criteria- level of responsibility, years of experience, education & training, successful track record and personal skill set. Don't forget, you get what you pay for!

113. Photo Bombs

The Purpose
Memories are some of the most valuable treasures your pastor has. Make a special memory for him by coordinating a church-wide picture day!

The Plan
Work with your pastoral staff to put together a "Picture Day" at your church! Give people a chance to take pictures of themselves with your staff, and with each other. Also, arrange for someone to take a picture of the entire group outside. The photographer will need to shoot the pic from a high vantage point to get everyone in the pic!

The Place
There are a variety of ways to make this fun experience a reality. You might opt for one use cameras, and have people take their own group or family pictures. You could invite people to take pictures with their smart phones or personal cameras, and send the digital copies to your pastor. Still another option would be to use a services like Instagram, Imgr, Flickr, Photobucket or Shutterfly, as well as websites like DropEvent & or LifeTouchEvents as a place for people to upload their pics.

The Price
A special way for you to commemorate this event is to pay to have a high quality picture printed of the entire group, frame it with a large matte and quality frame, and have everyone who was present sign the back of the picture or the matte frame!

114. What's Behind Door #3?

The Purpose
Everyone loves gifts! Everyone loves surprises! So why not merge the two? It's like your own church version of a game show! Only on this show, everyone is a winner!

The Plan
Choose three fantastic gifts- a day at the golf course with carts… a weekend getaway with their spouse… a shopping spree at a sporting goods store… tickets to the concert of the year… WHATEVER! Put one gift behind each door. Number the doors. Then have staff draw a number. You decide if you want to allow then to "steal" a prize already chosen, or if they end up with the luck of the draw!

The Place
Doing this during Pastor Appreciation Month, and celebrate the creativity and uniqueness of your staff!

The Price
These prizes can be fairly expensive, so make sure you either have a group of people that will donate these, or that the church Personnel & Budget teams had the forethought to budget this in for the year!

115. Picnic Basket in the Park

The Purpose
Nothing says relaxation like a picnic basket and a lazy afternoon in the park! Let your pastor enjoy a wonderful basket packed with love, and the time to enjoy it with his family!

The Plan
Buy a nice, large basket designed just for carrying picnic lunches to the park. Who knows, you may be helping your pastor start a wonderful family tradition! Pack the basket with a delicious lunch for him and his family! Make sure it's a lunch that's easy to eat at the park (spaghetti is probably NOT a good idea)! Lunch could be something you prepared, or had catered. Also hand him an inexpensive backpack that has a Frisbee, a set of horseshoes, a picnic blanket and maybe even a Bluetooth speaker that he can play tunes through with his smartphone!

The Place
It would be helpful if you've scoped out a good park, and maybe even made a trial run to make sure it's clean and will be a fun experience!

The Price
You could easily spend from $50 to $150 on this event, but with the memories that will come from this event, that's a total bargain!

116. There's a Gorilla at the Door

The Purpose
Everyone ought to have a singing telegram show up at their home or office at least once in their life! Nothing competes with having a gorilla or a life sized chicken serenading you!

The Plan
Call around to several professional services to get bids on what it would call to hire a professional. You might even consider skipping the professional, renting a costume and doing this one in person! Be sure and videotape the song and response and post it on YouTube or your church website.

The Place
The more public the place, and the more people there are to enjoy this event, the better it will be! It's probably not a good idea to hiring a singing juggler to show up right before the morning sermon though! However, showing up just as staff meeting begins, or at a church fellowship or special group fellowship would be fantastic!

The Price
Singing telegrams can cost from $50 to $500 dollars, so let your fingers do the walking, and Google search until you find a bargain. A free version of this is available if you have a crazy uncle who has a gorilla costume and loves to show out!

117. Calgon, Take Them Away

The Purpose
Even pastors could use some pampering and some tender, loving care! Can't you just picture him with cucumber slices on his eyes, an oatmeal & yogurt facial mask followed by a mani/pedi and topped off with a relaxing Swedish massage?! As crazy as it sounds, he might just love it!

The Plan
Do your homework, and get prices on various services in your area. You may have a local spa that covers all of these, or you may opt for a more expensive option of shipping him off for a day to a nearby luxury hotel with spa accommodations. Really want to make his week? Send his spouse along with him so they can enjoy the spa experience together!

The Place
There are plenty of smaller, locally owned spas that can offer most of the services mentioned. For the sake of time, this may be your best option. Still, it won't hurt to at least check on the prices to send him and his spouse away for a day of pampering before you choose!

The Price
Spa treatments vary greatly in price. Any one of the items above could cost from $30 to $100 apiece, so choose what fits your budget best!

118. Surprise!

The Purpose
So much of the life of a pastor and family is built around a regimented schedule that involves church services, appointments and meetings. A little (planned) spontaneity can be just the thing to stir things up!

The Plan
You want this to be a surprise as much as is possible. Use your detective skills to make sure that they actually do have the evening free, and that it's something that will work. Once you've discovered what you feel is a fairly open evening, make your plans, and plan on giving them about an hour notice to get ready!

The Place
For your fun night out, make it something special! Choose a dinner theater, a murder mystery or a fun night around the hibachi chef table complete with flaming onions and a crazy chef slinging knives around in the air! Just make it fun, and a night they will remember! Only one rule for the night—NO church talk!

The Price
Plan on spending $30 to $60 per person. This night isn't about eating a Happy Meal you bought with a coupon! Splurge a little and have a great time!

119. It's a Fiesta

The Purpose
What's better than a great dinner at home? A great fun dinner at home that someone else bought, prepared and delivered to show you their love!

The Plan
This is a fun experience to build a theme around! Why not make enchiladas, tacos and nachos… and provide bandito mustaches and sombreros for everyone to wear during the meal! Or choose BBQ, baked beans, potato salad and all the fixins' for a Cowboy dinner, complete with cowboy hats and bandanas!

The Place
The great thing about this event is that you're taking dinner to your pastor in a place where they truly can relax- HOME! Since you're technically inviting yourself to drop by their house, you should call them a week or so ahead of time! Ask them what night would be best, and then get busy!

The Price
Dinner can be picked up at a restaurant, or prepared by you and your family as an extra special way of showing your love and appreciation! Don't forget that if you're adding any decorations for your themed dinner that the cost for this event will go up!

The Icing on the Cake! Open Your Wallet Up Wide

120. A New Chair

The Purpose
Your pastor most likely spends a bulk of his work week in his office, and while he's there, his tush is planted in his office chair. You can make sure that his workday is comfortable with a new and great looking office chair.

The Plan
Determine what your price range is, and then stop by your local office furniture or warehouse store, and pick up one of their catalogs.

The Place
It will be awesome if you can let your pastor pick out is own chair. Gift wrap the office furniture catalog, and present it to him as a gift! Let him know what price range he can be searching through, and send him on his way!

The Price
A nice office chair can be fairly pricey. Costs range anywhere from $150 to over $500. Remember, this is more than a piece of decorative furniture. This chair will last for years, and it will provide comfort while he studies, and can even impact the quality of his health. Don't be cheap!

121. Date/Family Night Out

The Purpose
Sometimes pastors need a little push (or maybe a big push) to make some time to spend with their spouse or with their family. Help him remember his priority to shepherd and to build a life of memories with his own family.

The Plan
This is a fun event, whether he opts for a romantic date night with his sweetheart, or a fun packed night out with the family! Date night might include a romantic dinner in a dimly lit restaurant and a stroll on the waterfront. A night on the town with family could include go karts, miniature golf or even a painting or cooking class with the whole group!

The Place
That little push we talked about... its two fold. First, put together a brainstormed list of options for your pastor, for both a date night and a family night. Second, make sure he knows that whatever he picks is paid for. No arguments.

The Price
Nights like this can stretch out the billfold. That means they can be expensive! $100 to $250 is not an unrealistic bill for the evening, so make sure you either get budget approval first, or find several families or a church small group that want to chip in and cover the cost as a group.

122. A Lamp Would Be Cool

The Purpose
Many churches have space that goes unused. Wouldn't it be awesome to create a "Pastor Cave", a really awesome office with all the amenities, something that would make him so excited to come to work!?

The Plan
Secure permission for the space first. Then add a nice desk, internet access, comfortable desk and lounge furniture, a stocked mini-fridge and maybe even a basketball goal on the wall!

The Place
The "Pastor Cave" ought to be someplace unique and set apart from the rest of the offices. This is a "special" place, reserved as an incentive to work toward, and a reward for exceptional service! Share the love, and spread the use of the Pastor Cave around your staff!

The Price
Furnishing this office will be fairly expensive. Look for discounts or donations of quality furniture to offset this set up. You might also consider spreading the cost of setting up this space over a period of time. Without donations, you might expect to spend $500 to $1500 dollars.

123. Don't Forget the Lighter

The Purpose
Who knows whether your pastor is a country music fan, a jazz man or a fan of that good old time rock & roll? He might even like Christian music! Tickets to his favorite artist or band in concert could be the highlight of his year!

The Plan
After you find out who his favorite bands are, spend some time on the internet reviewing their concert schedules in the coming year. Choose a venue close to you, and buy the bet concert ticket seats you can find!

The Place
More than just getting him a set of tickets, check into the possibility of backstage passes, or even a shout out to your pastor during the concert!

The Price
Tickets and a backstage pass can set you back $100 to $500. If the concert isn't local, you'll need to cover travel, and maybe even meals and a night stay in a motel. Be sure to throw in money so he can buy a t-shirt or a CD as a memory!

124. Donate To Their Cause

The Purpose
Most pastors have a soft spot for agencies and causes that ease suffering and help hurting people, whether those causes are inside the local church or not. He would be totally blessed if you or a group of friends made a significant donation in his name to his favorite cause!

The Plan
Investigate and discover what his pet cause is… or just ask him outright! Most people who support a charity or special cause are very willing to talk about it!

The Place
If you want to make the best impression with your gift, wait until you can show up at a fundraising event for his cause, and bring your check with you to present to him at the event.

The Price
One way to multiply your gift is to find local businesses that might be willing to match any gifts that are made. If you know some business owners, approach them with that idea! Then take your gift, and the matching gift from business owners to his event. If you can muster up an individual or group gift that totals $1,000 or more, you'll have touched his heart in a way most other gifts can't!

125. Baseball Cards or Star Trek

The Purpose
What is your pastor's hidden hobby? Is he a closet Trekkie? Maybe he's been collecting comic books, stamps or Cabbage Patch dolls for years? Everybody loves something, so find out what he collects, and help him collect some more!

The Plan
After your "hobby snooping" has paid off, and you know the things that your pastor loves, take your time and look for the best you can find, at a bargain price. Knowing specifics in this area is critical. If your pastor collects Superman comics, even the best Incredible Hulk comic is not going to impress him. Buy smart, but look for the best prices.

The Place
Take your pastor to lunch or dinner, and find a way to bring up the topic of his collecting hobby into the conversation. Once you get him all worked up and talking incessantly about his hobby, pull out your special gift and make the presentation!

The Price
Lunch or dinner could be $40 to $75 alone. Collectibles vary greatly in price, but you might spend anywhere from $75 for a special baseball card, up to $500 or a $1,000 for other collectibles.

126. It's An Original

The Purpose
A walk through your pastor's office, or a quick conversation with his spouse can reveal what your pastor enjoys in the way of art. He may be a western art buff, or love sculpture. He might enjoy ocean scenes or abstract art. Find a spot on his wall or coffee table and fill it up! An original work of art in his favorite genre could be just the ticket!

The Plan
This gift may take some time, especially if you are having the original piece of art special ordered for your pastor. You can hire an artist to create this "one of a kind" piece based on your pastors' tastes.

The Place
Have a special event where you are able to do an "unveiling" of this special piece of art. You might consider inviting your pastor and family to dinner at your house, and after dinner and before dessert, make a special presentation.

The Price
Share the cost of this work of art with several other families. Privately commissioned artwork can cost from $500 to $5,000 dollars, so make sure this is something you can afford, or that you have others willing to help you split the cost on this art!

127. Helmet Head

The Purpose
Your pastor does so much for your church and for the people who make up the church family. Great sermons, spectacular fellowship events and going above & beyond in a variety of different ways! He's the quarterback of the team, and when he's doing well, the team wins! Reward the quarterback!

The Plan
Find out your pastors' favorite football team, and order him a full sized football helmet with the team logo. You can find these in a number of online stores. Also order a variety of sport decals. Check out www.sportdecals.com or www.healyawards.com for their selection!

The Place
Make a fun presentation of the helmet to your pastor, and let him know that from time to time there will be awards of various decals. To spice this up, present a helmet to each of your pastors, and watch the competitive spirit for decals kick things up a notch! Decals could be awarded for best Halloween costume, best Chicken dance, or even for years of service! The only rule about decals is that it has to be fun!

The Price
Football helmets can run from $300 to $500 apiece. Decals are fairly cheap, running from $2-$10 each for standard decals, up to $.22 cents per decal for custom decals, but with a minimum of 200 decals ordered.

128. Life Coaching

The Purpose
Sometimes the shepherd needs a little shepherding of his own. Life coaches can come alongside your pastor as an encourager, counselor and advisor.

The Plan
Talk with your pastor before moving forward with this choice. Some pastors may be a little apprehensive about pursuing this, so by involving he in the discussion before hiring one might minimize any concerns he might have.

The Place
Take your pastor to lunch, and during your conversation bring up the idea of a life coach. Ask him if he's ever considered it, and if he would be open to it. Life coaching might involve encouragement with his marriage, parenting skills, time management or dealing with stress. Suggest all of these as possibilities.

The Price
Life coaches vary greatly in cost, based on their training & experience. The going rate for life coaches varies from $75 to $200 per hour. Determine how many hours you are willing to cover based on the best rate you are able to negotiate.

129. Basket Weaving is Nice

The Purpose
Pastors stay fresh in ministry when their minds stay sharp. One thing that helps a mind stay sharp is to learn new things! Offer to pay the tuition for a class or training event, something that has absolutely nothing to do with ministry or his role at the church!

The Plan
Investigate what's available in your area. There might be painting classes, dance classes, cooking or welding classes available in your area. Build as large a list of opportunities as possible, and then meet with your pastor to let him pick his experience!

The Place
Call your pastor and invite him and his spouse to dinner one evening. While you're there, pass the list to them and invite them to choose something they would love to do, either individually or as a couple!

The Price
One night events might be as inexpensive as $50 per person, or as expensive as $250 apiece. Don't let cost be a determining factor in their choice, so when you print the list, don't include the cost for their viewing!

130. Call the Limo

The Purpose
Typically a pastor will be worried about driving a car that is "too nice", over concerns that members of the church might think he's being proud, or worse yet, making too much money! Take that worry away, and rent him the car of his dreams for a week (or at least one close to it!)

The Plan
Find a way to dig into his inner "car beast"... talk to the other pastors, or some of his friends in the church. Surely he's shared his love for mustangs, or his desire to have a convertible or muscle car. Then get to work looking for one that you can either borrow or rent for the week!

The Place
Invite your pastor to a special lunch at his favorite restaurant, and offer to meet him there. Pull up in his special ride for the week, and after lunch invite him to check out your special ride. Then spring the good news on him that this ride is HIS for the rest of the week! Another spin on this gift might be to rent a limo to take your staff and their spouses out for a night on the town!

The Price
This gift could be free if you own or can borrow a car from a church member for the week! If not, the car rental or limo could cost from $75 to $200 per day! Still, it will be worth it when you see his eyes light up!

131. Mama Needs a New Pair of Shoes

The Purpose
The old saying, "Ain't nobody happy if Mama ain't happy!" is a wise proverb! One of the kindest things you can do for a pastor is to bless his spouse or family! It's time to go shopping!

The Plan
Part of the fun of shopping for most women is not just the purchase, but the entire shopping experience! You might want to consider involving two or three of her closest friends in this shopping spree! They can buy their own stuff, but they are there to help her shop and celebrate her finds as she makes them!

The Place
If you know or can discover where your pastors' wife loves to shop, then buy her some gift cards to those locations! You don't want a gift of cash to go to pay bills that she feels are more important than a new pair of shoes or a new outfit!

The Price
Make the trip special, and worth the time! Whether you are sending her shopping with cash or with gift cards, plan on spending between $150 to $300 on this day on the town!

Alphabet Soup- Attitudes That Feed Their Soul

Admire Them

Pastors are typically encouragers by nature. Turn that around, and let them be the receiver of your admiration. Pinpoint something you admire about them. Share your honest admiration with them, and let them know you appreciate them.

Be Available

Ministry can be a lonely profession. Pastors feel an unrealistic need to be strong for everyone else. That makes it hard for them to ask for help, or to let down their guard. Tell them you're there if they have anything they want to talk about, and that anything they share will be kept in confidence.

Brag, Brag, Brag

Everyone, including pastors, need to hear that they are doing a good job. Brag on him in front of your friends & at your workplace. Be authentic in your compliments, and don't wait for a situation to present itself where you can brag—make it happen!

Challenge

Pastors are leaders. As such, sometimes people can be intimidated by them, and afraid to challenge them. Encourage them to try something you know they want to try, but haven't yet because they're scared. Over lunch, ask him how many free evenings he has each week to be with his family. If it isn't enough considering the age of his children and the needs of his wife, engage in some straight talk about the pace he keeps.

Compliment
Make this a regular habit. You won't over inflate his/her ego by doing so. If they serve regularly, then pick out something they do exceptionally well, and point it out. Pick a personality trait like staying calm under pressure, or a skill like being an effective communicator.

Courtesy Counts
Sundays are the busiest workday of the week your pastoral staff. Tons of people pulling at them for their attention or information. Believe it or not, some will hold onto their complaints or criticisms until Sunday so they can launch their verbal assaults in person. A word of encouragement here. Have something to complain or criticize just before worship? Don't.

Encourage the Encourager
Keep your eyes and ears open to subtle signs of discouragement or sadness. Even pastors can have downer days. If you see something that causes you to think they are in the dumps, then encourage them... and then encourage them again.

Family Time
The multitude of church events, counseling sessions and worship services can overpopulate a family calendar to the point a pastor's family never sees each other. Use whatever influence or persuasion you have to make sure your pastoral staff spend quality and a large quantity of time with their own families.

Focus, Grasshopper
Your church has a ton of activities going on. Busyness can become the business of the church if the church and staff aren't careful. Help your pastor stay focused on the big picture, and you do it to.

Fresh Start
Your pastor is NOT going to be like the last pastor. This can be especially difficult if the former pastor was endeared to a large segment of the church family. Toss out the Cookie Cutter –Don't expect him to be just like the last pastor.

Grow Personally
Want to do something fantastic for your pastor? Then grow personally in your faith. Deepen in your personal relationship with Christ. Share the gospel with the lost. This can affirm your pastor more than you know.

Honor Guard
Think about something very specific that your pastor has done, said or lived that made an impact on your life. Take the time to share that with them. Beyond that, honor them and the role the serve in your church and in your life.

Insightment
Thank your pastor for sharing a fresh insight on Scripture, introducing you to a new way to look at things, or opening your mind and heart to new opportunities for service.

Inspiration Instead
If they inspired you to push outside your comfort zone, thank them for inspiring you to take a risk, and let them know how it paid off. A much better path than criticism or busyness.

Intentional Introductions
Introduce them to someone who may challenge them and help them grow, as they've done for you. Sometimes it's hard for pastors to build relationships outside their church family. Be that catalyst in his life.

Invitations Home
Invite Them to Your Home. Your pastor and his family need a church that loves them. But what matters more is having people, families that actively show them they are loved. Invite them to your place. Show some love.

Listen Authentically
Fully listen to what they have to say, instead of forming your rebuttal in your head and waiting to speak. Learn to quiet not only your mouth, but your mind as you listen. Don't listen, waiting for your turn to speak. Listen to learn, and listen to grow.

Love Deeply
Love your preacher into greatness. Sometimes a pastor needs a good friend to dream for him, when he's having trouble dreaming for himself. Love your pastor into greater service and growth than he believes is possible.

Lower Expectations
Lower the expectations on his kids and spouse. The church needs to be a safe place not only for your pastor, but for his family as well. Living in the ministry fishbowl is a lot of pressure. Lower the level of expectations!

Loyalty Matters
Commit to stand with him through tough times. He needs to know that he can trust you, and that loyalty is a two way street.

Offer Silence or Stillness
If you don't have anything good to say, then be quiet. Sometimes your pastor may just need someone to go hang out with at the fast food restaurant, or go fishing. No talking, just being there.

Patiently Offer Patience
Be Patient and Understanding. Sometimes the church life is a volatile one! Be the voice of reason and calm that brings some peace to his life and ministry.

Praise Publicly
Praise them in a review on Yelp and/or recommend them to people you know. It takes very little time to write a glowing personal review for each of your pastors on Google.

Pray Persistently
Dedicate time to pray for your pastors each week, but let them know what you are specifically praying for. Better yet, ask them personally how you can be praying for them, and ask them on a regular basis.

Passionately Protect
If you find yourself in a group and the conversation turns critical toward your pastor, purposefully say something encouraging.

Reasonable Expectations
Realize that your pastor is not superhuman. Your pastor has the same kind of family, financial and personal stresses you do. You do him a great service by reminding others of this as well.

Recognize Regularly
Have a recognition Sunday where special groups, individuals and the church as a whole recognize the pastoral staff member. Cards, gifts, a dinner, roast, or any fun activity you can imagine!

Respect Office & Personhood
Respect his leadership. You may not always agree. That's ok. Being ugly, hateful or undermining his role as pastor is not ok.

Responsive & Open
Be Openly Responsive. When you step out, whether it's in service, worship or leadership, you encourage his heart.

Serve Alongside
Go to your pastor and ask him where you can assume a position of responsibility. Much of the work of a pastor is to "equip the saints for the work of the ministry." Step up and do your part.

Stop Gossip
Stop gossip. It's that simple. When you hear it, stop it. Ask people not repeat it. Be the place where gossip stops.

Submission is Strength
Submit to the Leadership of your Pastor. God has places him as the spiritual shepherd of your congregation. That doesn't mean he is a dictator, but it does mean he is worthy to be treated with honor, and following his leadership. If you are unable to do so because of theological or moral reasons, either step aside or move on.

Trust Dangerously
Give Him the Benefit of the Doubt. Your pastor deserves your respect, and he needs your support, even when you don't know all of the facts.

Understand His Heart
Know that your pastor is sold out to following God's will, and seeking His leadership in everything he does. Before jumping to conclusions about his motives or decisions, remember his heart, and how he's proved himself worthy of your trust.

Voice Your Support
Look for public opportunities to voice your support and respect for pastor. It could be in small group sessions, church business conferences or in public at a meeting outside your church.

Welcome Him Regularly
Your pastor needs you. Find him every Sunday, and let him know that you're more than just glad to see him. Tell him how happy you are that he's your pastor, and how much his friendship means to you.

Xpect The Best
There will be those who question some, much or all of what your pastoral staff does. Be the person that believes the best, works for the best and expects the best from your pastor!

Yank Their Chain
In addition to being your pastors' biggest fan, from time to time he will need people who will be totally honest with him. That means telling him privately what he needs to hear, even if it's not something he wants to hear.

Zip Your Lip
When you don't have something supportive to say, then why not try saying nothing at all!

www.ingramcontent.com/pod-product-compliance
Lightning Source LLC
Chambersburg PA
CBHW071922290426
44110CB00013B/1444